KURT HANSON

THE

BLACK

SKYGOD

A MEMOIR

FORWARD BY:
DAPHAROAH69

Kurt Hanson

Creator, Writer and Copyright © by Kurt Hanson, 2025 Editor,
Book Format Artist and Advisor by:
Larry C. Wilson, Jr. (Dapharoah69)
Additional Editing by: Umer Muzaffar
Book Cover by Kurt Hanson & Umer
ISBN #979-8-218-83207-0
PRINTED IN THE UNITED STATES.
Hardcover Version

The Black Sky God
A Memoir

PAN AM
TWA
DELTA
DELTA
NORTHWEST
My 4 former airlines
TWA
TRANS WORLD
PAN AM

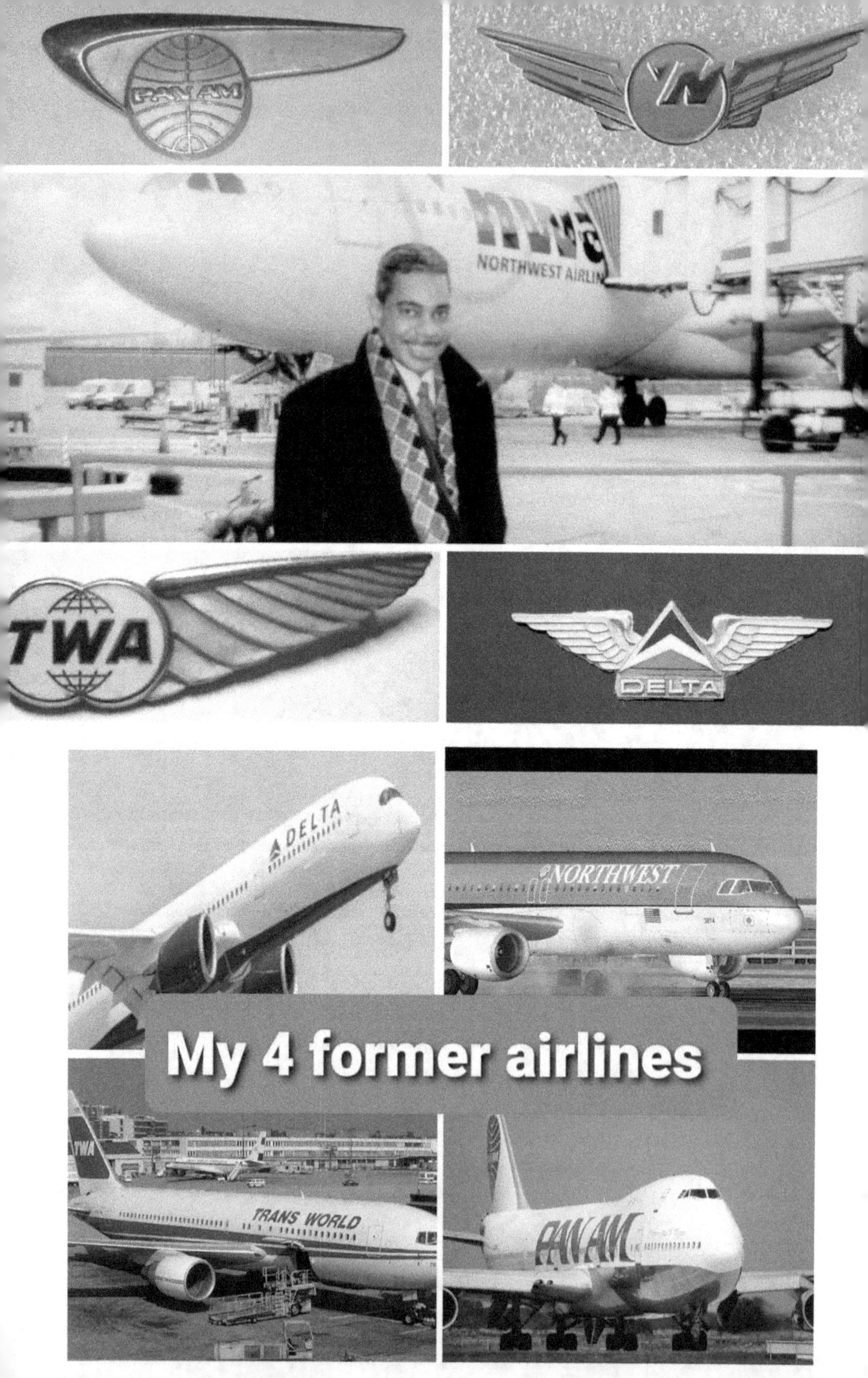

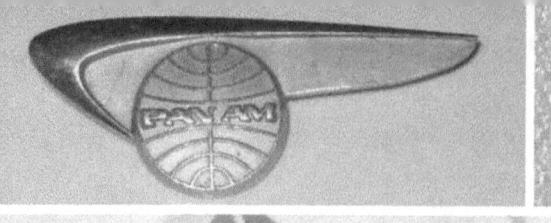

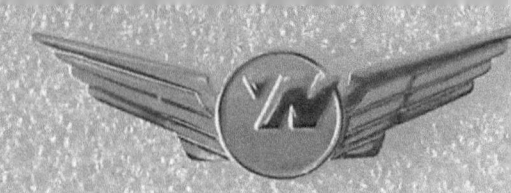

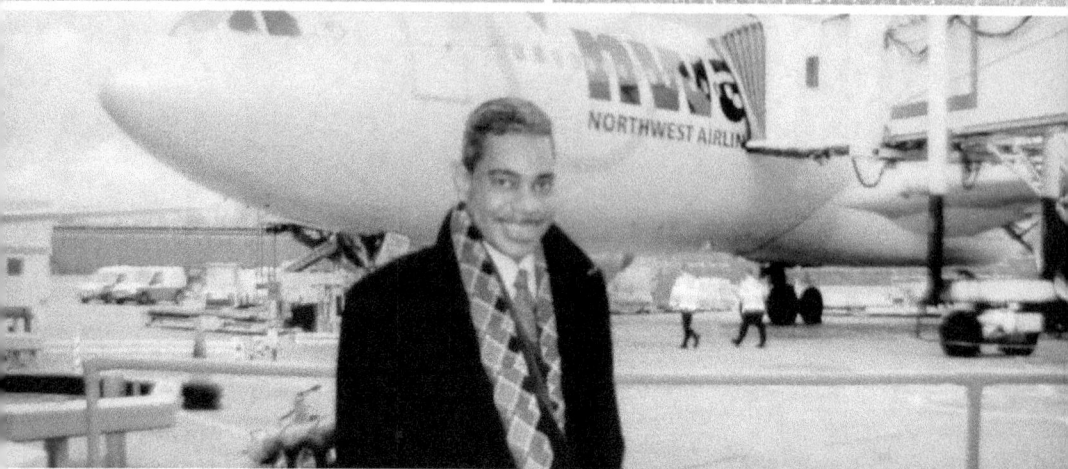

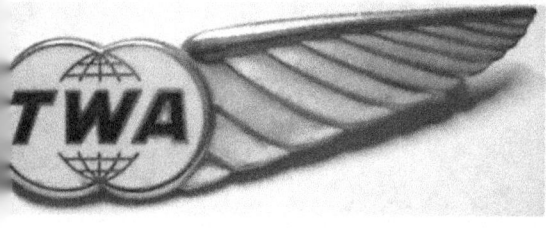

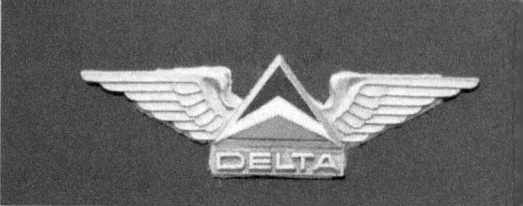

DEDICATION:

Jacqueline Williamss
E. Lynn Harris (1955-2009)
The late Congressman John Lewis
Dr. Joan Muir..
All the male flight attendants worldwide..
And to the real Niklaus VanBuren (1962-2021)

LOVE
HAS
NO
LIMITS
ONLY
PEOPLE
DO

THE BLACK SKY GOD

TABLE OF CONTENTS

AUTOBIOGRAPHY

KURT

THE BLACK SKYGOD

THE MOST DEVIOUS AND MISCHIEVOUS FLIGHT ATTENDANT AT 35,000 FEET

2 | The Black Sky God

KURT HANSON

The Black

Skygod

AN AUTOBIOGRAPHY

4 | The Black Sky God

FORWARD
BY DAPHAROAH69

FIRST EDITION

Photo courtesy of Sergey Yusin and Dapharoah69

Award-winning, bestselling author of "Call Her Queen Hatshepsut"
and "The Law of Beasts Book 1 – Act 1," Stellar Business
Award 2024 recipient for Best Publishing in Florida, Life-time achievement award in
Storytelling, 2024, and Certificate of Recognition from the New York State Senate,
2016

I'VE KNOWN KURT HANSON, WHO I affectionately refer to as my "dad,"
for over a decade. Growing up without a father was challenging, so
meeting him warmed my heart because he was filled with love, honor
and intelligence. We spent a lot of time together, along with my
spouse.

We previously worked on a book project back in 2015,

when I wrote the sequel to my mentor E. Lynn Harris's "Basketball Jones." Imagine my surprise to discover that Kurt was the original AJ Richardson from the book, and that he gave the storyline to E. Lynn Harris.

It was a full circle moment for me. Kurt is an amazing person. He gifted me and my spouse John our first stay at the famous Ritz Carlton hotel in Atlanta, Georgia.

He also surprised us by giving us a tour of a condo E. Lynn Harris gifted to him as a thank you for allowing him to use Kurt's life with an NBA player as the basis for "Basketball Jones."

I was already an author before Kurt and I crossed paths, and once we did, he has been a beacon of light in me and my husband's lives for over a decade.

When we met, Kurt was a distinguished gentleman and well cultured.

The way he walked, spoke and carried himself reminded me of someone brought up with class and decorum, because his kind I'd never encountered before in my entire life.

Inevitably, we lost contact, and it destroyed me to learn that dad lost everything he ever worked so hard for and was left with nothing.

It greatly pained me to learn that his deceptive family

defrauded him and sold both of his homes from under him.

When Kurt found me again last year, it was a tearful moment because dad learned that he never lost me or John. We will always support him and have his back.

When he approached me to edit his autobiography, I didn't hesitate.

When I published my first book back in 2004, when I was homeless and at my lowest, I reached out to so many authors to help me, only to be denied.

I was rejected by publishing houses, so I did it on my own and landed my first three books on the Barnes and Noble.com Top 100 bestseller's list at the same time in February of 2009, while I was homeless with no marketing team, promotion or million-dollar agents.

I was among the first self-published authors to achieve that feat. Since so many people denied helping me, I wanted to be the author that said "yes" to any African-American that needed help publishing their books.

I went a step further by showing them how to cut out the middleman and become their own publishers, controlling their own voices. I did that free of charge.

I did all the editing, book formatting and polishing for those authors, giving their books the same love I gave myself.

Kurt's life is extraordinary. Editing his memoirs took me through a flurry of emotions.

From the fires of his past to the disappointment he suffered from family secrets hidden from him, to how he discovered his birth mother, Kurt's journey is both spectacular and inspiring.

To rise to success and to hit rock bottom, and rise again from the ashes into a beacon of light, his story will touch the lives of anyone who has been burned, betrayed, robbed of their possessions by family members or anyone who experienced the highs and lows of love.

It was an honor to edit and format dad's book. May Kurt's autobiography inspire you, the reader, to look deep within your heart and souls and find your peace and protect it at all costs.

It takes guts and courage to be an open book and share your life with readers, and the fact that Kurt wrote his memoir on his own says a lot about the man he has become. May you, the reader, be inspired by Kurt's journey.

To Kurt, dad. I'm so very proud of you.

For years you watched your son, ahem, me, win awards after awards and grace front covers of national and international magazines after being denied and told my books weren't good enough two decades ago when I was homeless, eating out of garbage cans to nourish myself.

Now, Kurt, you are a published author.

Thank you for trusting me to maintain your voice and polish your heartfelt words.

May you continue to succeed and touch the lives of anyone that has gone through similar trials and tribulations that you've endured.

"The Black Sky God" is a testimony, not just a book, that I recommend to anyone that wants to know what loving yourself looks like.

May this testimony inspire many to tell their own stories, their way, controlling their narratives and protecting their voices.

I hope you continue your writing journey, dad. May you write many books and watch the seeds of your labor sprout and replenish everything that was selfishly taken from you. You aren't a victim, you are a victor, a survivor and a testament to love, grace and sustainability.

May your family be proud of your perseverance. May God continue to use you as a vessel to help others.

Your humbleness and your genuine heart need to be studied in college classrooms all over the world, because you, dad, are the Holy Grail of success in my eyes.

I love you, always and forever.

Warmly,

Your son, Larry C. Wilson, Jr.

Bestselling author Dapharoah69

Preface:

"THE BLACK SKY GOD," a memoir about the highs and lows of Kirt Hanson's extraordinary life, are deeply rooted in truth, but his journey has many layers. Roughly ninety percent of his heart-felt words happened exactly as he has written, yet certain details have been altered to shield the identities of people who may still be alive.

Some of the chapters have been heightened or dramatized. It's not to deceive anyone, but it captures the fire, the scandal, and the danger of what it felt like to live through such difficult times.

This is not a courtroom transcript. Controlling his narrative, he is a survivor that has endured without apology. Some secrets will stay buried...for now. And remember, this is just a fraction of his story.

He wanted his readers to get a glimpse of the glamour, the chaos and the costs of his prestigious flight attendant uniform.

This book may be one of a kind, but it is only the tip of the iceberg. This is the Band-Aid covering his wounds...

Yet some scars don't heal....

AUTOBIOGRAPHY

5.0 RATING
★★★★★

THE BLACK SKYGOD

THE MOST DEVIOUS AND MISCHIEVOUS FLIGHT ATTENDANT AT 35,000 FEET

KURT

Jacque Williams wrote: "This book is absolutely captivating — I couldn't put it down. The author takes you on a remarkable journey through his life from infancy to age 60, filled with raw emotion, family drama, scandal, revenge, and unbelievable twists. I found myself laughing, gasping, and even crying, especially during the heartbreaking moments with his grandmother.
It's an engaging, easy read, beautifully complemented by numerous photographs featuring the author and well-known celebrities, which brings the story to life even more.
This is truly a MUST-READ from beginning to end. Once you start, you won't want to stop."

Eduardo Simurg wrote: "The Black Sky God is unlike anything I expected. Hanson takes something as familiar as a flight and twist it into a strange, mischievous world full of personality, humor, and sharp insight. There's a spirit in this book — playful, rebellious, and a little dangerous — that kept me reading."

ABOUT THE AUTHOR:
Kurt Hanson is an ordained Minister, trained Baritone singer. A graduate of the prestigeous Jamaica College and the Sorbonne University in Paris, he also holds a Master's in Communications. He has flown with Pan Am, TWA, Northwest and Delta Airlines serving NBA and NFL players, the White House Press Corps and Military Charters. He speaks 3 languages and has traveled to over 100 countries in his 30 years as a flight attendant.

THE

BLACK

SKY

GOD

Kurt Hanson
Northwest Flight Attendant Graduate
April, 1999

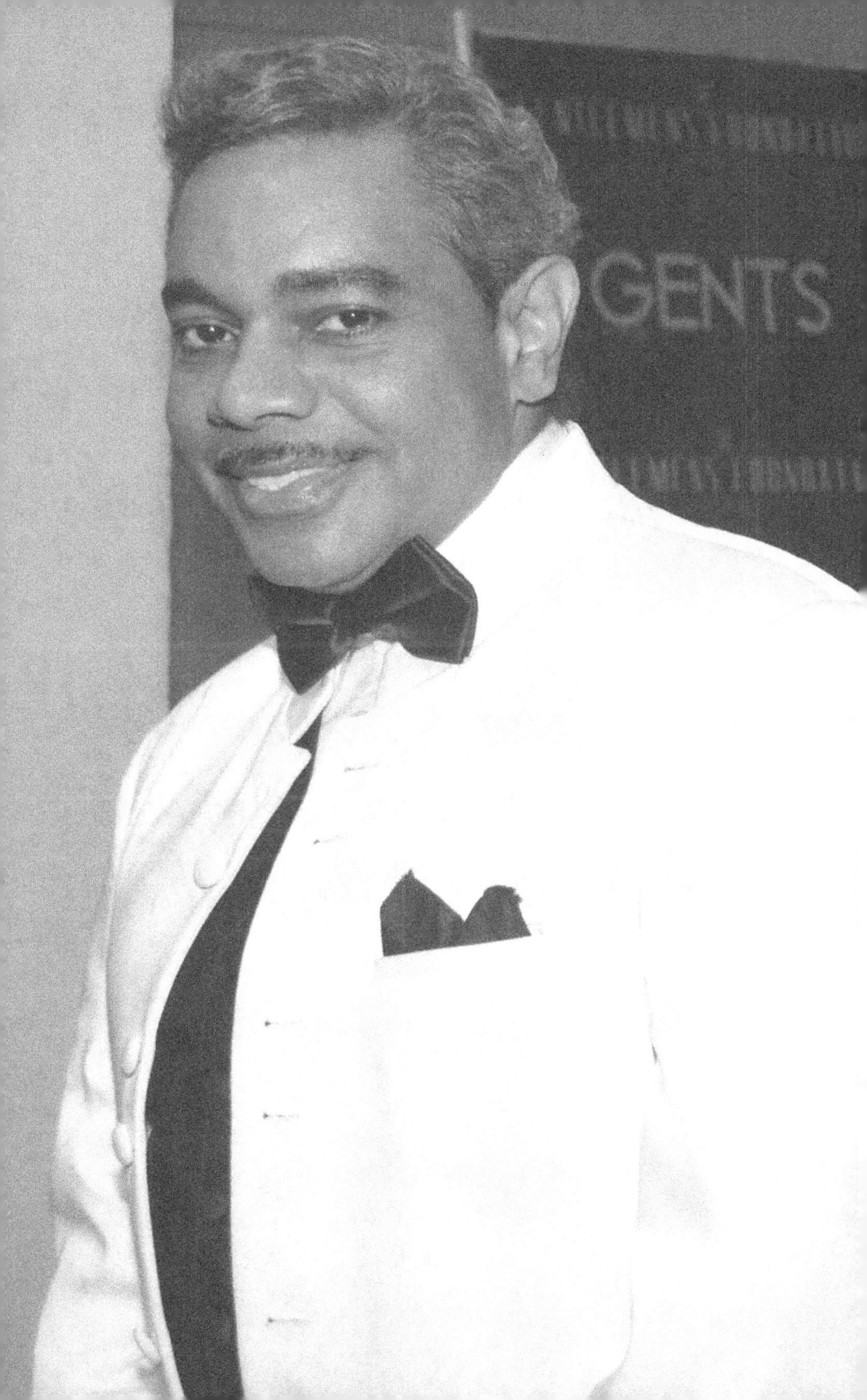
GENTS

"I survived because the fire inside me burned brighter than the fire around me." — *Unknown*

I have fought the good fight
I have finished the course
I have kept the faith

PRELUDE

Critical Care

A SECURITY GUARD SPOTTED ME. HE TOOK ONE look at my uniform and assumed I was American military. I didn't correct him. I didn't have time.

"Ward 30. Critical Care."

He took me there himself. Inside, the air was too cold. My flight bags hit the floor at the nurses' station. An older woman looked up. "Mr. Anderson...Oh my! You look just like your picture. Your grandmother raved about you. She's been showing everyone your flight attendant graduation photo. She couldn't wait to come visit you."

With a soft voice, I told nurse Jackson about my last conversation with grandma. "She told me she was having a little pain in her stomach. What happened?"

The light dimmed in nurse Jackson's eyes. "Your

grandmother was in far more pain than she let on. The doctor ran some tests, and when they came back strangely abnormal, he decided to open her up. But as soon as he did, he saw it: gangrene. It had already taken over her abdomen. He made a larger cut, and... it was everywhere. There was nothing he could do but stitch her back up." I staggered back like she had physically struck me.

"She went into a coma this morning," she continued. "That's when we called your mother, but your grandmother had already asked for you. She wanted you here."

"Can I see her?"

She led me down the hallway. I braced myself with every step. There, tucked in the corner of the ward, was the woman who had given me the love my parents never did. Tubes snaked from her frail body. Machines hissed. I stood still, breath frozen in my throat. "Talk to her," she whispered. "She can hear you."

I took grandma's hand. It felt like paper. "Grandma... it's me, Kurt. I came as fast as I could. I was in Germany."

Immediately, the heart monitor spiked...

1

Excuse Me, Fritz

As the sun began to rise over Kingston, Jamaica, a frantic flight attendant rushed through the airport terminal like assassins were after her. Her heart hammered from anger, pain, and the bitter sting of betrayal. Filled with emotional upheaval, Enid had just returned from maternity leave before her world was destroyed.

It was a challenging time because *today* was the day she would confront the man who had destroyed her life.

Her ex-lover, Fritz, a pilot, would be navigating the Pan American Airlines morning flight from New York's JFK to Miami International Airport.

After ten years of marriage to a stunning beauty queen turned diplomat, he never acknowledged their affair or the child they had together.

Enid kept her pregnancy a secret. The shame and heartache festered like an open wound without anesthesia.

But now, she was going to expose him with a few simple words and a letter.

As she approached the aircraft, her heart continued to pound in her chest. A whiff of booze funneled up her nose from Fritz's breath.

A surge of vindication coursed through her veins.

He climbed into the cockpit, bleary-eyed from last night's indulgence.

It was time to take some action.

"Excuse me, Fritz," she said firmly, her voice steady. "You can't fly the aircraft in this condition."

He glared at her. "Get out of my way, Enid."

"No," she stubbornly insisted, stepping forward. "You're unfit to fly and I'm reporting you."

Annoyed, he narrowed his bloodshot eyes. "I'd like to see you try, Enid."

"Be careful what you ask for, Fritz. Your wish is my command!"

Within moments, the airport manager was notified, and Fritz was escorted off the plane. His face was a mask of shock and fury.

Little did he know, while his career hung in the balance, the consequences of his actions were about to deepen in ways he could never imagine.

Later that day, Enid found herself standing at the threshold of her own turmoil. She had devised a plan. She didn't want the child. A baby was a constant reminder of Fritz's betrayal. She was moving to the United States, and she couldn't take the baby. Fritz did want a son, so maybe he'll take him.

With no way to change the past, she ensured that her baby would be left at his father's mother's doorstep. It was cruel, but it was also a way of reclaiming power over her shattered life.

About a week after he was fired from Pan Am airlines, she was on her child's grandmother's doorstep still dressed in her flight attendant uniform. Unlike Fritz, she still had her job. Her hair was in a tight bun. Despite her inner rage, her make-up was flawless. After knocking, the door opened to reveal Beverly, the housekeeper.

She was clad in a chaperon apron and a hat, like those French maids. When she saw Enid with the baby, she excused herself and went to get Fritz's mother, Leila Louisa Mason, affectionately called "Aunt Lou."

She was a poised and sophisticated woman whose grace could only be matched by her wealth. As she approached Enid and the baby, she asked "What brings you here, Enid?" Her voice was laced with concern.

Enid swallowed hard, forcing her emotions down. "I have something for you," she said, handing over the bundle wrapped in a soft blanket. "This is Fritz's baby."

As Aunt Lou gasped, Enid felt a rush of satisfaction mixed with guilt. "There's a letter for you to give to Fritz and his wife. It explains everything."

With that, Enid turned on her heel and walked away, leaving Aunt Lou to cradle the child and the weight of the revelation that would soon shatter their lives.

2

The Unraveling

THE EVENING SUN DIPPED BELOW the horizon as Fritz stumbled through the door. He was still reeling from Enid humiliating him at his place of employment. The nerve of the selfish bitch. Yes, he may have hurt her beyond logic and reason, but that was no excuse to put his livelihood or his job in jeopardy. Come to think of it, he was terminated. As a result, he turned to excessive drinking, hoping it would drown away his problems, but they only intensified. He hadn't yet heard about the baby.

With a strange expression, Aunt Lou approached him. The anxiety in the air was palpable.

"Fritz, there's something you need to see."

"What now?" he snapped. His temper was already frayed from the horror of what transpired this past week.

With trembling hands, Aunt Lou handed him the letter.

"It's from Enid."

Angrily, he ripped it open. The contents tumbled out like a whirlwind of chaos. Each word sliced deeper than the last. Her betrayal, the child, and her intent to leave unnerved him. Fueled by alcohol and a lifetime of repressed emotions, rage surged through him.

"Is this true?" he bellowed, his voice echoing through the lavish home. "You let that woman deliver our child?"

Aunt Lou placed a calming hand on his shoulder. "Fritz, you need to understand—"

But his arrogance was insatiable.

He couldn't bear to face the consequences of his infidelity. He staggered toward his mother, and balled his hands into tight fists. At that moment he struck her. In utter shock, she staggered backwards.

"That baby is not mine!" he shouted, collapsing into a drunken stupor. "I don't want it!"

As the night deepened, his wife, Norma, returned from a

diplomatic function. The atmosphere shifted. Aunt Lou's expression spoke volumes. Fritz was too far gone in his inebriation to even notice his wife's concern.

"Fritz, what happened?" Norma asked, with panic rising in her voice.

In a moment of desperation, Aunt Lou handed Norma the letter. As she read it, her heart raced. Nauseous, she experienced a mixture of disbelief and denial that bubbled deep within the pit of her stomach. Her finger weakened, and the letter slowly fell from her grasp. "You cheated on me?" she demanded.

He laughed derisively. "Don't act surprised, Norma." "What do you mean by that? You're the one that had a baby out of wedlock. You did this to us, so you can shove your attitude up your ass."

"That's real classy coming from you."

"Answer my damn question," she said intensely. "You know I can't be tied down."

"Who are you trying to convince? Me or your selfish ass?"

"I'm telling you how it is." he said.

"You are so full of it."

"Listen closely. In any event, you weren't able to give me what I really wanted: a child."

"Well, it looks like you have one now, scum!"

Deeply hurt, she got in his face. The confrontation escalated quickly.

Their words were like blows; the verbal abuse became physical, and in that chaotic moment, Norma realized she could no longer live in a cycle of betrayal and violence. He was not the man she married and vowed to love forever. The next morning brought clarity. After a sleepless night, Aunt Lou and Norma sat down to discuss the fate of the child. They both agreed about one thing. The baby would not suffer for Fritz's sins.

(Norma and Kirt)

3

A New Dawn

MONTHS HAD PASSED, AND THE legal documents were finalized. The child was registered as the legal son of Norma and Fritz Anderson, with a new birth certificate issued. Despite their dysfunctional marriage, Norma grew to love Kirt.

She was determined to provide stability for the child.

As the years unfolded, Norma grew stronger, eventually divorcing Fritz after years of abuse.

Aunt Lou became the boy's primary guardian. She showered him with love and luxuries. Truth be told Aunt Lou was a godsend and very hands on in her grandson's life. They moved into a lavish estate, and the boy grew up blissfully unaware of his tumultuous beginnings.

At eleven, he began his formal education at Jamaica College, an elite institution known for producing leaders. As he stepped through the gates, he felt the weight of expectations but also a thrill for the opportunities that lay ahead.

However, the darkness loomed, and the whispers of his past

followed him. Unbeknownst to him, his biological mother had not forgotten.

Enid had settled in the United States. Her heart was still heavy with regret and unresolved feelings. As she watched the news from afar, a familiar face emerged. It was a photograph of her child, thriving in a world that she had abandoned.

The best and worst were yet to come. The truth lingered on the horizon. It was poised to reveal the complexities of love, betrayal, and redemption.

The boy's journey had just begun, and the path ahead was littered with challenges that would shape his identity.

As the new school year approached, change was in the air. Unbeknownst to him, the storm of his origins was about to clash with the life he had known, bringing everything he had ever known into question.

4

Allow Me To Introduce Myself

MY NAME IS KIRT ANDERSON. In 1962, I was born of Jamaican parentage in a country on the verge of independence, yet still deeply influenced by its colonial past. My family was anything but ordinary. My father was a pilot for Pan American World Airways.

It was a career that placed him in the elite circles of international travel.

He was a disciplined and ambitious man. He always dressed impeccably in his uniform, commanding respect wherever he went. My mother, on the other hand, was a force of nature. She was elegant, strategic, and socially astute.

A former Jamaican beauty queen, she later rose to the ranks of diplomacy, becoming a consular general in Germany.

But the true pillar of our family was my paternal grandmother, Louisa Mason, affectionately called "Aunt Lou."

A gracious woman with a heart of gold, she was a rare white Jamaican, a descendent of Scotland, who invested in real estate before Jamaica gained independence.

She had accumulated significant wealth and, more importantly, influence.

She'd helped raise me. She always showered me with love, attention and gave me anything that I wanted.

She was the undisputed matriarch. And

in our family, her word was law.

5

The World Beyond Jamaica

MY EARLY CHILDHOOD WAS SHAPED in England, where my father was based for work. England in the 1960s was a place of strict order, formality, and racial tensions simmering beneath the surface.

My father's profession afforded us a level of privilege, but even as a child, I sensed the underlying expectations placed on me.

I had to be well-mannered, articulate, and aware of my surroundings at all times.

Meanwhile, my mother was building a career in the diplomatic world.

She was based in Germany, and I would spend time with her when I wasn't with my father in London.

My mother moved with an air of sophistication. She effortlessly charmed her way through political and social circles. I watched her closely. I studied how she smiled just enough, how she tilted her head slightly when speaking to men, and how she never revealed too much.

Even at a young age, I absorbed those lessons.

I was unaware that they would later shape my own approach to relationships and human dynamics in a way that would make or break me.

Or maybe both.

6

A New Reality

AT THE AGE OF 10, MY WORLD changed. My grandmother decided that I should return to Jamaica to live with her. It was not a request, mind you. It was a decision made for me, and I had no say in the matter, even though it was my life.

I had grown accustomed to my structured life of England and Germany, but Jamaica was an entirely different world.

And I wasn't sure if I wanted to be there. Not

that I had a choice.

My grandmother's house was grand. It was located in one of the more affluent areas. She ruled it with an iron thumb, ensuring that discipline and respect were upheld at all times.

There were house staff, extended family members coming and going, and an unspoken understanding that I was being groomed for something greater.

I just didn't know what that was.

While my family was wealthy and powerful, Jamaica in the 1970s was a nation undergoing a noticeable transformation.

The energy was electric, filled with both political unrest and cultural vibrancy.

Reggae music boomed from street corners, political debates raged, and people spoke of a future filled with both hope and uncertainty.

7

Jamaica College

IN 1974, I WON A SCHOLARSHIP to Jamaica College. It was an elite all-boys school known for producing some of the country's top leaders. It was a place of tradition, discipline, and intense academic expectations.

From the moment I set foot on campus I knew that politics and the power dynamic was the gospel. Who you were friends with, how you carried yourself, and how well you navigated the social hierarchy said a lot about your character.

I didn't quite know how to cope with such biased bullshit,

but the road that lied ahead was an unpredictable journey.

Strategically, I gravitated towards the subjects I was the strongest i.e. language arts, history, literature, and geography. French, Spanish, and German came easily to me.

It opened doors to a world beyond the island and my mental capacity. History always fascinated me. It offered a deep understanding of power, war, and human ambition, but math and science were my mishaps.

I barely scraped by in Physics, Chemistry, and Biology.

I knew that no amount of tutoring would ever make me enjoy those subjects.

8

Awakening Desire

IT WAS AT JAMAICA COLLEGE THAT I first became aware of my attraction to older men. There were two in particular who captured my attention. One was my history professor. He was a former Nigerian football player, Ah! He was tall, commanding, and effortlessly charming. And the other male was the school librarian. He was a quiet yet authoritative man who also happened to be a Major in the Cadet Corps.

I was drawn to both of them in different ways. The professor exuded masculinity and confidence. His lectures were filled with passion. It was always my pleasure to attend them, studying the way his lips moved when he spoke.

However, the librarian was more enigmatic. His silence intrigued me as much as his presence did. An air of mystery surrounded him in ways that made me clutch my pearls.

To get closer to him, I joined the Cadet Corps. I damn well knew that my interest had little to do with discipline and everything to do with proximity.

At the same time, two of my classmates, Gary and Paul, both tall, athletic, and confident, caught my attention as well. I had attention deficit disorder when it came to gorgeous men.

Unlike my professors, Gary and Paul were within reach. They were males my age who were on their own paths to self- discovery. Yet, instead of pursuing them, I played a different game. I could be a crafty bitch when I wanted to be.

I avoided them. I pretended that I wasn't interested, causing them to chase me instead.

9

Mastering the Game of Attraction

WATCHING MY MOTHER COMMAND diplomatic circles with style and grace had given me a masterclass in subtle manipulation. She had a way of making men feel important. She offered just enough attention to keep them engaged while maintaining an air of mystery that drove them wild.

I took her techniques and refined them for my own purposes.

I learned how to charm men with well-placed compliments. If you blew smoke up any man's ass he'd swear he was Puff the magic dragon.

When a man spoke, I listened to him long enough to make him feel special. I would withdraw at the right moments to create curiosity. I acted older than my age. I was mature and painfully controlled.

The ability to make people feel like they were the center of my world became my superpower. It was the greatest tool I used to get what I wanted.

And what I needed, of course.

Unfortunately, power came at a price.

As my A-game became more intense, so did the stakes. Balancing academics, extracurriculars, and my carefully constructed web of relationships was exhilarating.

And, yes, exhausting.

10
School Life, Escapades and Virginity

Carolyn Allen with (L-R) Kurt Hanson, Hugh Japhatt and Kevin Sinclair in the LTM Pantomime, "Ginneral B"

ONE EVENING AFTER PRACTICE, I realized that it was extremely late. The tennis team had challenging upcoming matches; the basketball team was in the middle of their season, and the swimming team was about to start their season.

I couldn't care less. I really did have a crush on Gary, but I always thought he was arrogant and full of himself. He was a great swimmer and had won several individual and team awards, but there was always an unspoken bond between us.

I ignored him in class, the gym and the locker room. He was a cocky jock who always stepped out of the shower without a towel just to get attention. An attention whore he was, and baby, mine was undivided. For some strange reason, I just happened to have the locker behind him.

There was something I noticed on one occasion, and I wanted to say it out loud, but I remained silent.

Gary did not wear underwear, like ever. And his scrumptious dick was curved, like a banana.

I wanted to tell him so badly to go put on some underwear, but it would look like I was actually watching him.

After ignoring him for two years, he complimented me on one of my tennis shots while I was getting dressed. So, he did notice me. Of course he did, my name was Kirt. I was the crème de la crème.

Coyly, I looked at his naked body and said, "Thank you."

Surprisingly, he became quite talkative, and it puzzled me because I still thought of him as an obnoxious asshole.

Ugh! For the life of me I couldn't understand why I was getting aroused. If I was a woman, my panties would be wet. It caught me off guard like a deer caught in the headlights of a speeding semi-truck.

I didn't know why.

Maybe because he was also getting aroused. I avoided looking directly into his bedroom eyes while I continued to get dressed.

He desperately tried to seek some form of attention. Everyone else did that to him. Validated him. I moved different. I was cut from a different cloth he couldn't quite afford.

Agitated, he sighed. "Why don't you like me?" he asked out of the clear blue sky.

The question weakened my safeguard.

Reluctantly, I turned and looked at him. "Because you are too cocky for my taste, and you're also full of yourself. There, I gave you two reasons."

It dawned on me that I used the wrong word. "Cocky."

He looked down between his semi-muscular legs, then looked up at me. He burst out laughing.

"I can't help it if God blessed me."

"Cocky" was my faux-pas.

"You and your smutty mind." I responded, chuckling along with him. I was hot and bothered, but I played it cool with a poker face. I couldn't let the left hand know what the right hand wanted to do.

"Finally, I get a reaction from you."

I grinned. "You may be blessed, as you said, but that doesn't mean you know how to use it."

Oh, my goodness. What have I done? I just opened a can of worms that I know wasn't going to end well.

"Do you want to see how well I can use it?"

I didn't answer. Suddenly, he came closer to me. "Don't get scared now, Anderson. You gave me a challenge, and I am accepting it."

The smirk on his face grew bigger, like a Cheshire cat. Yes, I was curious but really, I was more talk than action. A dog with all bark and no bite.

"I won't hurt you. You don't have to be scared."

I looked at him, then lowered my eyes. This was getting serious. And judging by his mouth-watering bulge, I could see through his towel that his dick was serious too.

At what point did he wrap himself with a towel?

Once I was dressed, I closed my locker, and he closed his locker as well.

Eagerly, I waited for him to make his next move.

I wasn't about to jump the gun. What if he was playing a game of his own and was setting me up? The only way that I'd look like an ass is if mine was on his tongue.

The thought sent a chill up my spine, but not enough to stop me from seeing where this little rendezvous goes.

A few hundred feet past the swimming pool was an old building. No one knew what it was used for. Gary and I knew it was there, but we figured it was an old classroom from years ago.

Gary led me to a small door. Grabbing the rusty knob, he turned it and the door creaked when he opened it. Inside, there were old desks and chairs. There were also tools tucked away in the corner.

I figured he had been there before because he moved around in the dark with ease.

How many males have you brought here already, I wondered to myself.

Perched in an adjoining room was a mattress with sheets and two pillows on the ground. I stood there looking at him grinning while unbuttoning his shirt.

"So, I take it you have been here before?"

He smiled but never answered. As he was completely disrobing, he came up to me and started to unbutton my shirt. The adrenaline took over. I didn't want to do it, but at the same time, I did. Talk about indecisiveness.

After gazing into each other's eyes, getting lost in our irises, we laid down on the mattress. We talked a little bit. That was nice. He said that he had been wanting this moment to happen a couple of years ago, but I didn't give him a chance.

He also wanted to know why I ignored him over the years.

I don't chase anyone. I never responded.

Abruptly, he leaned over and kissed me. My nipples tingled as my lips did all the talking. He was soft and gentle. I'd never experienced anything this seductive in my entire life. Have I dreamed about it? Quite possibly. Had I imagined what it'd be like? Likely so.

After moving deep inside me, this was the day that I lost my virginity.

We had sex three more times and then just like that, boom, he and his parents relocated to the United States.'

So, there I was. I had slept with the Major/Librarian, the history professor and the captain of the swimming team. I had my fun, but it was all about to stop as I had some time to prepare for my big O'Level examinations.

11

Wine and Soft Jazz

As GRADUATION APPROACHED, I knew I had to make some tough decisions. The delicate balance I had maintained that fulfilled my needs was no longer sustainable. My relationships with my professor, the Major, and my two classmates had to end.

I had them all wrapped around my little finger. What no one told me was that they all had expiration dates in my life.

Nonetheless, I played tennis and volleyball for the school, so that brought a bit of notoriety and watchful eyes.

I attempted to withdraw from sports. I avoided conversations, and I didn't return phone calls. To my dismay, people just didn't let go of me so easily.

My indifference only made them more determined to win me over, like I was the grand prize in some unsolicited contest. It was a game I no longer wanted to play, but one I had started.

And now I had to finish it.

Mr. Mohammed and I had a bond. We were extremely close. When he taught me about his Nigerian culture, we were inseparable. I skipped classes or arrived late without facing any repercussions. He would sometimes give me a ride home after my tennis or volleyball practice, or after he finished basketball practice.

Then we deterred. I started going to his apartment just to be with him.

One memorable occasion, we had a relaxing evening with incredible wine and soft jazz.

I was very relaxed, absorbing his energy. We had a lot of things in common, and it catapulted us to a forbidden teacher/student relationship. We trusted each other.

He knew that our secret was safe with me.

12

Growing Fame

SUFFICE IT TO SAY, MAJOR BRYAN and I had a similar bond. He chose me to do a lot of his administrative work for the cadet corps. Maybe he appointed me, so I'd always be close to him. I didn't care, really. I did my job well. I was so proactive that it really impressed him.

With the Major, I was attracted to his status in the Army. His powerful, authoritative manner was so sexy to me.

The way he looked in his military uniform set me ablaze. Tell me, who could resist a man in uniform? Even though everyone called his sexuality into question, they still respected him.

So, you might be wondering if there was any sex involved? Yes, there was, but you'd just have to use your imagination. I could never kiss and tell. Not at age sixteen.

At the same time, I threw myself into my passions: singing with the Jamaica National Chorale, acting with the Jamaica National Theater, and playing a character in a popular radio series which aired every day.

My growing fame in the Arts gave me the perfect excuse to cut ties with those I had entangled.

13

Graduation and the Next Step

EXAMS WERE BRUTAL. I HAD to take eleven of them. I passed them all. I graduated with full honors. I excelled even beyond my wildest dreams. I passed my GCE O'Levels with distinctions, securing my place for the next stage of my education.

The next step was choosing where I wanted to go next. Since foreign languages were not offered in the 2-year 6th form course at Jamaica College, I was accepted at another school.

My headmaster set it up with the headmaster of Campion College.

Unfortunately, I had to leave Jamaica College and my skeletons behind.

Campion College was a school that offered foreign languages. It would be for the 2-year 6th form course, then I would be required to take the GCE Advanced level exams.

I felt like I made the right choice. It was definitely a fresh start for me in a new environment. It was also a new challenge.

But what I didn't know was that Campion College would not just be a new chapter.

It would turn my entire world upside down in ways I never could have imagined.

And I didn't see it coming.

14

Campion College and Enid

LEAVING JAMAICA COLLEGE FOR Campion College was a move borne of necessity. Jamaica College's prestigious reputation was undeniable, but its academic offerings were limited. Advanced- level foreign language courses were nonexistent, and my growing passion for languages needed more than the institution could provide.

Campion College was a world apart from the one I was raised in. It drew its student body from the elite ranks of society. There were children of diplomats, government ministers, business moguls, and local celebrities.

It was a glittering parade of privilege, influence, and opportunity. Yet, what I found most captivating was the sheer brilliance and ambition of my peers.

Though I was there primarily for the language program, I wasted no time immersing myself in the school's vibrant extracurricular scene. It was the drama club that truly captured my imagination.

They were in the midst of deciding what to do for the National School's Drama Festival.

Part of my studies in my French literature class was a book by a writer named Moliere. The title was "Le Tartuffe." It was about a man who swindled his way through a wealthy family. He lied his way from religious piousness to the man of the house.

Tartuffe made himself so valuable to the rich man, that he was named sole heir to the rich man's fortune while flirting with the man's wife and making himself indispensable.

I pitched the idea to the Drama tutor, and we wrote a play based on the character "Tartuffe." From that moment I stepped into rehearsals I felt the unmistakable pull of the stage.

By a stroke of good fortune (or my talent), I was selected to play the lead character. Rehearsals were grueling, but intoxicating, A thrilling rush of creativity enveloped me during my collaboration with my peers and drama teacher.

It was there I met a magnetic and playful girl named Simone Williams. Our chemistry was immediate, electric, and undeniable. Inevitably, she became my closest friend and confidante. Her presence wrapped itself around anyone she encountered.

Together, we conquered the festival. I won "Best Actor" and Simone won "Best Actress" for the entire national event.

That kind of recognition cemented our bond, turning our experience into a golden friendship, and our friendship into family.

But the most significant breakthrough came from a brief announcement made during one of my French classes.

The Jamaican Ministry of Education announced a competitive scholarship to study at the prestigious Sorbonne University in Paris.

Encouraged by my teachers, I applied with a mix of ambition and hesitation. I was aware that over two hundred of the brightest minds across the island would be vying for the same opportunity. Three weeks later, I was seated in front of a panel of interviewers. The questioning was relentless. They probed every aspect of my language skills, my aspirations, and my ability to thrive abroad.

When the results were finally announced, I could hardly believe it.

I had won!

Within days, the news spread like wildfire. Reports of my achievement appeared in Jamaican newspapers, as well as in publications across the UK, Canada, and the USA.

The phone lines at Campion were buzzing with calls from

journalists eager to speak with me.

Everyone seemed to want a piece of my story, but it was one phone call that changed everything.

15

My Who?

I WAS SITTING IN THE MIDDLE of a lecture when I was paged over the school intercom to report to Mr. McKay's office, the school Principal. What could it possibly be about? I was paged a couple more times. Wondering if it was another call from a reporter, I took my time.

When I got to the receptionist desk, the secretary told me to go straight into Mr. McKay's office. When I strolled through his open door, Mr. McKay had an unusual look on his face, like he was in a daze. He asked me to take a seat.

"Kirt," he began, his voice gentler than usual. "I received a phone call a short while ago. A lady called for you. She introduced herself as Enid. She said that it was important. I spoke to her for a bit before deciding to call you in here."

I frowned, and searched his face for clues. "What did she say?" The tension was thick and surreal. I almost laughed. This must be some sort of elaborate prank, but Mr. McKay's face remained serious.

His eyes were filled with of concern. "She's still on the line," he said. "I'm putting her on speaker so I can hear everything. I want you to listen to her with an open mind. As improbable as it may seem...I think she's telling the truth."

Slightly, my fingers trembled as I reached for the phone. Mr. McKay pressed a button, and suddenly, the woman's voice filled the room. "Hello..."

"Hello, this is Kirt. Who is this?"

Her voice was smooth, steady, and warm. "I just wanted to congratulate you on winning the scholarship. You've done something remarkable, and I couldn't be prouder of you."

"Thank you," I hesitantly replied. "But...who are you?"

She paused with a deep sigh. "My name is Enid Lewin. well, I am actually your birth mother."

The words hit me with a fist to my gut. "My... what?"

"I am your birth mother," she repeated gently. "I left you with your father and grandmother when you were only three months old. It wasn't by choice. I was forced to leave you, and I've regretted it every day since. I left you with your grandmother because I believed she could provide the stability I couldn't."

It felt like the culmination of everything I'd worked hard for was about to blow up in my face.

16

You're Fucking Kidding Me

I GLANCED AT MR. MCKAY, HIS expression unreadable but focused. His eyes stayed on me, watching carefully, almost protectively.

"Why are you telling me this now?" I asked, my voice cracking. "After all these years? And how do I know you are telling me the truth?"

"Your grandmother owned a home at 10 Foxlaw Avenue, by the Our Lady Of The Angels Catholic church. It was a blue home with a mango tree in the front yard, and the gate was painted white. Your Nanny's name was Beverly."

"I...I can't..."

"Also, you may know my sister Mrs. Ferguson who takes care of your grandmother when she visits the doctor. Listen, I've followed your achievements from a distance, Kirt. I've read about you, heard about you..."

"And when I learned about your scholarship," she continued, "I knew I couldn't stay silent any longer. I needed to tell you who I am. To let you know that I am proud of you. That I have always been proud of you."

My heart thundered in my chest like a wild, desperate wolf thrashing against its cage for fresh blood. My breath came in shallow gasps, and my fingers gripped the edge of the desk until my knuckles became numb.

I swallowed hard.

17

Grandmother's Number

EVERYTHING SHE SAID WAS TRUE. I did know Mrs. Ferguson. Truth be told, I always wondered why Grandma and Mrs. Ferguson always whispered when I was around. Enid described the house correctly and knew my nanny's name.

"So, you... you left me?"

"I didn't have a choice," she said. Her voice was laced with pain. "I was forced to leave you, and I have lived with that pain ever since."

My head was spinning. I needed answers. Real answers. Not from this stranger on the phone, but from the only person who had ever been constant in my life.

"I have to go now," I choked out, my voice brittle. Without waiting for a response, I hung up the phone.

Mr. McKay didn't stop me.

He nodded, as if to understand that the only place I needed to be was somewhere else.

I looked at Mr. McKay. He said he wasn't sure what to do but thought I should at least hear her out and form my own judgement.

He asked if I needed to call my grandmother and I said yes. My hands trembled as I dialed my grandmother's number.

18

True Confessions

SHE PICKED UP ON THE THIRD ring. "Hello?"

"Grandma," I said, my voice shaking with urgency. "Who is Enid Lewin?"

There was nothing but dead silence on the other end. It stretched longer than I thought possible, like a rope being pulled taut until it was about to snap.

"Grandma?" I pressed. "I am asking you a question. Who is Enid Lewin?"

A sound finally emerged. It was a low, furious growl. "Why the hell did that woman contact you?"

"So, it's true." The words tumbled from my lips, jagged and hot. "Everything she said is all true. My life...everything I've known... was one big deception."

"Sweetheart, listen to me."

But I couldn't listen. Not then. Not when the world I thought I understood had been ripped from beneath my feet.

I slammed the receiver down. I was angry, hurt, and betrayed.

My emotions collided in a chaotic, uncontrollable storm.

Everything had changed.

The visceral impact sent me spiraling.

19

Under My Sheets

I LOOKED AT MR. MCKAY AFTER he saw the look on my face. Quietly, I left his office feeling indifferent. My thoughts collided with each other with no sense of order or sanity. As I stumbled back to class, my classmates were a blur because I couldn't focus. Their laughter and chatter were reduced to muffled echoes.

My body was trembling. Every sound was amplified, distorted, a cacophony of anger, betrayal, and disbelief nearly took my breath away. I couldn't escape the word that kept echoing in my mind: *Mother.*

Enid. Enid Lewin.

It was a name I had never heard before and yet, suddenly, it meant everything to me. I purposely stayed out late that night. I decided to go to Mr. Mohammed's apartment.

After he welcomed me inside, I told him what happened. As I laid awake, with my head on his chest, my mind flashed through my memories. I tried to make sense of the impossible.

My grandmother's anger on the phone cut me deeper than a sword.

She had known all along.

All those years she was my world shattered. All those nights she'd tucked me under my sheets at bedtime dissolved into oblivion. All those times that she told me I was her precious boy was a farce. All the whispered assurances that I was loved beyond measure had all been based on a lie. It was all a lie.

When the sun began to rise, its light was cold and unnatural. I had to know the truth.

The full truth.

And if my grandmother wouldn't give it to me, I'd rip it out of her if I had to.

20

Protect me from what?

I DIDN'T GO TO SCHOOL THE NEXT DAY. I wasn't up to it, quite honestly. I wasn't a fan of strangers witnessing matters of my heart. Mr. Mohammed took me home early that morning and my grandmother was already up waiting for me.

"Where were you all night? You had me and your mother worried."

"Grandma," I said, my voice steadier than I expected. "I want you to tell me everything."

Reluctantly, she said, "Kirt, I don't think...."

"You don't think what?" I curtly interrupted. "I am sixteen years old! So, please! No more lies!" I snapped.

"I think you better tone it down before...."

"You've lied to me my entire life! Don't you realize that? "Am I supposed to know what you're implying?"

"Who the hell is Enid Lewin?"

The color left her face.

"And why didn't you ever tell me about her?"

There was a pause, so thick and heavy I could feel it pressing against my chest.

"I did what I had to do to protect you!" Her voice was hard, clipped, and stripped of its usual warmth.

I was annoyed. I could choke her, but I refrained. "Protect me from what? From the truth?"

She narrowed her eyes. "No. From her!"

The way she spat the words out caused me to flinch. "What do you mean?" I whispered.

"She left you. She abandoned you, Kirt. She walked away and didn't look back. I raised you. I gave you everything she never could. And when she showed up again, pretending to care, I sent her away. Because she didn't deserve you."

"But she is my mother!"

The words sounded foreign and tasted bitter, like aloe on my tongue. "She's the one who gave birth to me. Selfishly, you kept *that secret* from me. And I want to know everything!"

21

The Shattered Glass

MY GRANDMOTHER'S SILENCE WAS a slap in the face. When she finally spoke, her voice was raw with anger and fear. "Okay, Kirt. Since you want to know the truth, I hope you can handle it. You were three months old, Kirt. Three months. And she handed you over to your father like you were an inconvenience she couldn't be bothered with. I stepped in because *someone* had to. She would've destroyed you."

The conversation ended in a torrent of shouting, accusations, and finally, the shattering sound of my broken heart. I was breathing heavily. The air was suffocating me.

But the pain didn't stop there. It seeped into every part of my life. It poisoned my friendships and derailed my successes.

I returned to school for my evening classes. "Thank God I will be rid of all of them when I go to Paris," I thought.

I was in a weird mood. Even the brilliant and intuitive Simone could see that something was wrong with me.

"You're not yourself, Kirt," she said one afternoon. She glanced at me, concerned. We were rehearsing for an upcoming drama competition, but my performance was hollow. I delivered my lines delivered with all the emotion of a lifeless puppet.

"I'm fine," I snapped.

She stepped closer to me, refusing to be dismissed. "No, you're not. And you haven't been since... whatever happened after you got the scholarship. You barely talk to anyone. You're acting like the world has turned on you."

"Maybe it has."

"What does that even mean?"

"It means," I said through clenched teeth, "that I've been lied to my entire life. By the very people who were supposed to care about me."

Simone's expression softened with sympathy. "You need to talk about it. Keeping it all inside is only going to tear you apart."

But I couldn't talk about it. Not even to Simone. The wound was still too raw, too jagged. I couldn't make sense of my emotions. All of the hurt, anger, and betrayal swirled together until I nearly passed out like a drunk before an AA meeting.

And then there were all the phone calls. Reporters from every corner of the world still clamored me for interviews. What should have been a time of triumph and celebration felt like a sick joke. The scholarship to the Sorbonne, once my crowning achievement, was now stained by the truth of my origin.

Mr. McKay wanted to talk to me, but I wasn't up for it, but he was my headmaster, so I couldn't avoid him.

"Are you okay?" he asked.

"I guess so Mr. McKay. Um, I would rather not talk about it. I need to focus on getting ready for Paris."

"I understand," he said, "But you know my door is always open."

He gave me a fatherly look with a small smile playing in the corners of his lips.

I started avoiding Mr. McKay's office. Stopped taking calls. Stopped attending interviews. Even when he cornered me a few days later in front of his office, I couldn't bring myself to explain. "Kirt, you've been through something difficult," he said carefully. "But running away from it won't help. Whatever you're feeling, you have to face it. You are a mature young man whom I admire a great deal, and your level of maturity is phenomenal." But how could I face something I didn't even understand? How could I reconcile the life I'd known with the brutal, shattering truth of my birth?

All I knew was that everything was tainted.

Weeks went by. Every day was heavier than the last. The world seemed duller. My victories were tarnished by the lies that my grandmother told. And still, the questions haunted me.

Who was Enid Lewin? How did she find me?

What kind of woman would abandon her child and then suddenly reappear, expecting everything to fall neatly into place?

And why, after all this time, did she find me?

22

Lies and Manipulation

I HAD DISCOVERED THE SHOCKING truth about my birth mother, Enid Lewin, during a phone call arranged by my headmaster, Mr. McKay, at Campion College. Enid revealed she was my birth mother and had left me with my despicable, lowdown, bitch-ass, no-good father and grandmother when I was three months old due to being forced to do so.

Grandma confirmed the revelation with anger, leaving me feeling betrayed, hurt, and confused.

My rage was volcanic. It bubbled up from somewhere deep inside, an anger that had been simmering unknowingly for years. Everyone had lied to me. My grandmother, the supposed matriarch, who ruled the family with an iron grip, had held this secret all my life.

My disgusting father, distant and unreachable, and the woman I had called mother for the past sixteen years could all go to hell.

All of them had kept it in the dark. And this woman, my

biological mother, Enid (a stranger until that very moment), was the interruption of everything.

I wanted nothing to do with any of them. All I wanted to do was to pack my bags and leave, to run as far away from my family as soon as possible. The scholarship to the Sorbonne was now more than just an achievement; it was my ticket to freedom.

Paris represented a clean break from all the lies and manipulation. I made a vow that day that once I left for Paris, I wouldn't speak to anyone in the family again. The wounds were too deep, the lies too corrosive.

If they didn't want me to know the truth, then I could live my life without them.

23

The Great Betrayal?

THE WORLD AROUND ME COLLAPSED in an instant. One phone call. One revelation. That was all it took to rip apart the very foundation of my existence. Was I overreacting? I didn't think so. I was not who I thought I was. My mother was not my mother. My cousins, my aunts, and my uncles had all known.

Every one of them had carried this secret like a delicate glass ornament, terrified that if they let it slip, it would shatter. But it did shatter. And I was the one left bleeding from the shards.

I stood frozen in place. The letter in my trembling hands unnerved me. My acceptance to Sorbonne should have been the most thrilling news of my young life. It should have been the gateway to adventure, to a new world of endless possibilities. Instead, it became my lifeline. My escape.

The walls of my childhood home, once warm and familiar, didn't feel the same. I could still hear their voices—the laughter, the conversations, the casual deceit.

How many times had they looked me in the eyes, knowing they were living a lie? How many times had I called a woman "Mummy" who never bore me, never brought me into this world?

I couldn't stay. Not for another moment.

I didn't say goodbye. I didn't give them the satisfaction of a confrontation, explanations or apologies. They had their chance to be honest, and they had squandered it. I packed what I could carry. I clutched my acceptance letter to my chest like a sacred promise. This was my way out.

Paris wasn't just a dream anymore. It was salvation. It was distance. It was a place where no one knew me, where I wasn't someone's secret.

As the plane lifted off the runway, I didn't look back. Jamaica was my birthplace, but it was no longer my home.

24

The Journey to Paris

FROM THE MOMENT I BOARDED the plane, I was so excited! A whole new frontier took on an entirely new meaning. I was electric, ecstatic and elated. All at the same time. Flying first class from Kingston to London Heathrow was a decadent experience. I absolutely loved it. I felt I belonged in first class instead of coach because I was the only one of my kind, I deserved it. I wasn't the coaching type, well, it depended on what I was into.

I had white tablecloth service, crystal glasses, and the kind of pampering that made me feel like royalty.

Yes!

Oh, yes!

I could get used to this!

The thrill of crossing the Atlantic on an aircraft that took me away from the only home I'd ever known, knowing I was leaving behind betrayal and heartbreak, only intensified my anticipation.

New horizons glittered on the threshold of the start of my independence, and baby, I was ready for it! I wanted it all.

Once I arrived at London Heathrow airport, I transferred to Air France bound for Paris' Charles de Gaulle Airport. The flight attendants spoke in elegant, fluid French. It was a language I would soon be mastering myself. Everything about the journey felt like a dream. Was I, though? Dreaming? Or was this a gateway to a new life free from the chains of my devastating family secrets.

Would Paris welcome me within the confines of all its chaos and beauty? Or would Paris spit me out and tell me to go back to where I came from?

The city was alive, vibrant and buzzing with energy and I buzzed right along with it. *Bon jour, Paris!* If my constant smile was the light then in that moment, I was the sun. However, navigating the labyrinthine Metro system with my hastily scribbled directions proved to be a challenge.

In fact, it annoyed the hell out of me.

A bit frustrated, I dragged my luggage up and down stairs like I was pulling a dead body, dodged the hurried Parisians that were somewhat rude as hell, and stumbled through broken French speaking civilians trying to ask for help.

What a waste of time.

Thankfully, the directions were clear enough, though they seemed more like a puzzle to solve. I looked for the train station within the airport, and from there, I made two transfers to reach my new home: a student dormitory at the heart of Paris.

It took hours before I finally found my way to the university. From the moment I stepped off the plane and into the bustling expanse of Charles de Gaulle Airport, the world had opened up in front of me.

Gone were the limitations of my past, the expectations, the tangled relationships, and the familial burdens.

This was my chance to become something I had only dreamed of, away from the heavy shadows of Jamaica and the life and family turmoil I was born into.

This new journey was going to shape the person I was

becoming.

With that, my spirit gradually started to decline. Yes, I was excited, but I was also confused. I wasn't sure if I would make it, but I pressed on. It was fueled by a combination of curiosity and youthful confidence.

Nonetheless, I almost got lost looking for my destination, but it didn't matter. Every wrong turn led me to a new path, and every misstep made Paris feel a bit more manageable.

When I arrived on campus, my heart pounded like pistons. I broke out into a huge smile. Inevitably, I was greeted by thirty- five of my fellow classmates. They were from every corner of the globe. One by one we introduced ourselves, yet I was still trying to catch up with everything happening around me.

Orientation began shortly after. I was alert and attentive. I quickly learned that my time there at Sorbonne University would not be a casual walk through the park. The next three years would be an intense, rigorous, and unyielding experience.

No breaks. No

easy days. Sigh.

Yet, this was the kind of challenge I had always craved.

25

Bonjour Mon Ami

MY INDEPENDENCE WAS STARTING to take shape. With that freedom came a new kind of responsibility. Gauland, from the Mauritius Islands, my roommate, was one of the students I met.

Immediately, we hit it off. Gauland was an easygoing, friendly guy. In his own special way, he made Paris feel less daunting.

He was already settled into the dorm, and I was grateful to share this new chapter of my life with someone so different from myself.

Together, we took our first tour of Sorbonne University. It was a place with rich history. With its grand library, the iconic student lounge was a place I would soon spend countless hours studying and reflecting. *And,* as I would come to discover, drinking wine and listening to the Beatles were some of the perks.

The lounge quickly became a regular haunt, but after some time I noticed something. The Beatles' "She Loves You, Yeah" was on repeat. I later learned that it was the only English album in the lounge, which explained its constant rotation.

Also, I soon realized that I was surrounded by a mix of cultures. Students brought their own rhythms, their own dreams, and their own ways of navigating the world.

It was intoxicating. The first piece of advice we were given during orientation was practical.

Manage your finances.

26

To My Surprise

WE WERE ALL RESPONSIBLE FOR OUR OWN spending, which meant that the bulletin board at the dorm became a lifeline. It was plastered with opportunities for part-time jobs.

The one that caught my attention was at the House of Chanel. This Sorbonne's special program was prestigious. We were training to become United Nations liaison officers.

My classmates were from every corner of the world, each one a rising star in their own country.

Our books, food, and accommodations were all covered by our scholarship, but personal spending money was up to us to generate.

In the student lounge, I looked over the bulletin board filled with job postings.

I read the requirements for becoming an usher for the House of Chanel, including preparing the fashion show venue and seating glamorous attendees.

Ugh! The pay was low, but the allure of the fashion world was irresistible.

I applied anyway. To my surprise, I was interviewed, and I was hired. It was there, among the glitz and the glitter, that I met Thierry Mugler. He was already a fashion icon. We worked well together, and he helped me learn the real Parisian French.

Our connection was instant.

I knew he was a great designer, but I had no idea that he would later go on to build his own empire.

But those early days, as I watched the models strut down the runway, were unforgettable.

It was a world far removed from the challenges I had left behind, and yet it felt like I was finally standing on my own.

27
Life At The Sorbonne

MY DAYS WERE CONSUMED BY grueling study sessions. Sorbonne University's rigorous reputation was no exaggeration. They worked straight through summer and winter breaks, translating between French, English, and German for eight hours a day. The workload was crushing, designed to break all but the most determined.

Yet I thrived.

When I wasn't immersed in books and studying for exams, I was enjoying moments of camaraderie with my classmates.

We played badminton, tennis and board games on the university grounds and retreated to the student lounge, where The Beatles' music played so often it became the soundtrack of our lives. We went exploring and even dined on the Bateaux Mouches.

On one occasion we held a cultural talent night.

I played Bob Marley with a mop on my head for dreadlocks.

My days were spent in translation labs, converting French into Spanish, Spanish into German, and constantly refining my linguistic skills.

If I wasn't studying or working, I was wandering the streets of Paris. I soaked in the sights and sounds of the city. I never once thought about Jamaica, nor did I long for the life I had left behind.

There was no time for the ghosts of my past to haunt me. I shuddered, thinking about it.

28

Take Chances

THREE MONTHS BEFORE GRADUATION, the university hosted a Career Day. Companies came to recruit students for internships and jobs.

The recruiters were a mixture of corporate suits and curious young professionals. There were companies like Air France and British Airways, but one company stood out: Pan American World Airways. Yes, that Pan Am. It was the same company my father was fired from for being intoxicated. How ironic.

For half an hour I had a conversation with the recruiter, and then another conversation with someone from the Pan Am flight attendant department. And she interviewed me in French to make sure I was qualified to be a French interpreter.

It was the most engaging interview I had ever had. By the end of it, the recruiter handed me his business card, along with a letter of understanding. He told me that if I graduated and secured a work permit for the USA, I would be offered a job.

I was elated. This was the break I had been waiting for.

I shared the news with my lifelong friend, Simone. She now lived in New York.

She encouraged me to come stay with her, to make the leap and pursue this opportunity.

I also reached out to my Uncle Roy. He reassured me that he had the connections to help me get the necessary work papers.

I didn't ask questions. This was a time to take chances, to trust the people around me, and to make decisions that would shape my future.

29

Au Revoir Paris

BY THE END OF THE PROGRAM, ONLY sixteen of the original thirty- five students had made it through. I graduated with honors. I was also valedictorian. It was a moment of triumph I would cherish forever.

When graduation day arrived, I held my diploma in my hand. It was a symbol of everything I had worked for, and everything I had left behind.

Paris had given me the independence I needed to break free from the chains of my past, and now, it was time to take that next step.

I boarded a plane to New York with a visitor visa in hand, ready to face whatever came next.

I smiled as the aircraft thundered into the air. Looking out of the window, I closed my eyes and slowly inhaled.

I was no longer the person who had arrived in Paris, uncertain and burdened by the weight of the past.

I was someone new.

And with that, I said goodbye to Paris, to the Sorbonne, and to the life I had once known.

The future was now mine to create.

30
A New Identity, A New Life

THE MOMENT I DECIDED TO STAY IN the United States, I knew I was walking a tightrope above a pit of uncertainty. The path to a U.S. citizenship was riddled with barriers. I didn't have any conventional means to survive. I didn't have a green card, sponsorship, or family connections. If I wanted to seize the opportunity Pan Am dangled like a carrot before me, I would have to be cunning, resourceful, and fearless.

My research began in the dimly lit corners of the university library. I poured over every document on immigration law I could find. I listened keenly to the stories of fellow students who had managed to remain in foreign lands despite the odds. I soaked up all the information like a sponge.

They told me about work visas and student visas. Some of them had gotten married for a green card. Others had found obscure legal loopholes, and a few had simply overstayed their visas, gambling with the risk of deportation.

Each option had its cons, but one thing was clear.... I needed paperwork, and I needed it fast.

I entertained the idea of a convenience marriage with Simone. It was a common route for those in my predicament. I knew people who had done it successfully, some even falling in love with their paper spouses. But finding the right person to trust with such a gamble was a challenge in itself.

Then there were the more daring methods. Could I acquire documents through less-than-legal means? I had heard whispers of forged paperwork, of people who knew people who could make problems disappear with the right amount of money.

It was a tempting thought.

With time slipping away, I weighed each option carefully, knowing that one bold move could secure my future or send me into a spiral of consequences.

31
Let The Games Begin

THE GAME HAD BEGUN, AND I WAS determined to play it well. The life of a Pan Am flight attendant or "steward" as they were called in the 1980s was within reach. They were glamorous, adventurous, and limitless and I was all of the above.

The next steps I took would define the rest of my journey.

I had set my sights on the American dream, and nothing was going to stop me.

Like so many others chasing "The American Dream," I arrived in the United States on a visitor's visa. My plan was simple. I would explore opportunities, and hopefully build a better life, but my uncle had a different idea.

He had connections. Yes, he knew people who could make things happen, for a price of course. Nothing was for free, unfortunately.

The cost was steep, but the promise of a new life outweighed the risks.

A birth certificate, a social security card, and a passport (documents that could make someone else) became my golden ticket.

The name on the birth certificate was not quite mine; it was a variation, a blend of fiction and reality. My date of birth was altered to match my mother's. Niklaus Kirt VanBuren It felt strange, yet liberating.

With my new identity, I stepped into the world of aviation, landing a job as a flight attendant with Pan American World Airways.

32

Hello Pan Am World Airways

THE AIRLINE INDUSTRY EMBRACED ME, and I, in turn, embraced the friendly skies. Over the next fifteen years, I built a career using this identity, moving from one airline to another. Each takeoff and landing was a step further from my past, and an investment in my future. I played the role well. No one questioned my credentials, but the truth lingered in the background like an undying echo.

Pan Am's training was no joke. It was less "glamorous airline orientation" and more "elite finishing school meets military bootcamp." We were flight attendants, ambassadors, safety officers, gourmet servers, and therapists in heels. And we had to look the part. Flawlessly. Every morning began with inspections. Nails had to be manicured. Shirts properly ironed and ties straightened. Hair properly in place. Shoes polished. No cologne stronger than a whisper.

We were walking billboards for an empire in the sky.

My classmates came from everywhere—California, Texas, Ohio, and even Europe. Some were debutantes looking for a bit of excitement. Others were adventurers, romantics, or rebels.

But me? I was on a mission. Every day, I trained like my future depended on it.

Because it did. And I loved every second of it. I had already told the class of my background with my father being a pilot in the early 1960's, and being the only black person in a classroom of forty other nationals, I was dubbed "The Black Sky God." This nickname stuck with me throughout my 30+ years of flying. There, among the starched collars and safety drills, I became someone new. Someone sharp. Someone untouchable. Everyone knew me as Kirt. I wasn't that boy from Kingston, Jamaica anymore, the one with the secret mother and the fictional childhood. I was poised. I was polished. I was Pan Am.

I'll never forget the first time I put on my uniform for picture taking. I ordered an extra photo for Grandma. She was right in the front row. With tears in his eyes, the gold wings were pinned to my chest by a retired captain who had flown with my father.

"Fly with grace," he said. "And never let them clip your wings."

I didn't.

33

Reporting For Duty Sir!

OUR FIRST PRACTICE FLIGHT WAS A SIMULATED run from New York to London. I balanced trays of filet mignon while reciting evacuation protocols from memory. I poured champagne with one hand while gently waking up a fake passenger slumped in his seat with the other. I walked that narrow aisle like it was my runway.

Pan Am was my freedom, my revenge, my rebirth. After graduation, I received my first assignment: a flight to Rome, Italy with a return through Miami. I wore my uniform like a king wearing his crown. When I walked through the terminal for the first time, little girls pointed. Men stood a bit straighter. Even the customs officers gave a nod of respect.

I had arrived. Not just in Italy. Not just in New York. But in the life I'd fought so hard for.

Thirty-five thousand feet in the air, somewhere over the Caribbean, I stood at the galley window, looking out at the clouds glowing pink with sunset, and whispered to myself: "This is what it feels like to be free."

I was barely out of training when I got a taste of the high life. My first few flights were the standard business travelers, honeymooners, and the occasional nervous flyers gripping their armrest like it was a life raft.

I was originally being groomed to work with the United Nations Liaison department, and never planned to become a flight attendant. In fact, it was the last thing I expected. But destiny had a funny way of showing me a world I never imagined; a world dripping in luxury, excess, and secrets so dangerous they could destroy empires.

34

"The Day the Sky Fell"

THE SADDEST DAY OF MY LIFE BEGAN at 36,000 feet, somewhere over Europe, with no warning. A sharp snap of a seatbelt and the hum of jet engines alarmed me as the world I knew began to unravel.

My grandmother wasn't just my heart, she was my everything. She was the woman who raised me when I needed grounding. When my youth teetered between uncertainty and chaos, she was there. It was she who told my mother and father that I needed stability and insisted they send me back to Jamaica.

And while my mother loved her deeply (she was a second mother to me, really) Grandma was the one who held the reins of my upbringing. She was present for everything: every award, every school play, every little triumph.

When I was hired by Pan Am, I didn't hesitate. I listed her as my stepmother just so she could receive free travel benefits. Of course, she never liked to fly alone. That meant I'd fly to Jamaica just to pick her up, then fly her back home when the visit ended. I never saw it as a burden. That was our ritual. That was us.

Most people didn't know what she endured every single day. After a tragic accident a decade earlier, she was left with a stoma. She was forced to do everything fecal through a hole in her abdomen.

The doctors in 1960 gave her a ticking clock, and told her she wouldn't live longer than three years. But they didn't know her. My grandmother lived with quiet dignity for nearly thirty more years, buying bales of cotton and girdles to manage it all, never once letting it steal her grace.

She was my birthday twin. My birthday was in January, and hers was the day after mine. We always celebrated together. Two Capricorns, two kindred souls, blowing out candles side by side was a beautiful thing.

She was more than family. She was a part of me.

In July 1987, she was set to visit me in New York for two weeks. I was living in the Bronx then, and she had her circle of friends in the city.

A week before I was due to fetch her from Jamaica, she mentioned some stomach pain.

"Go see a doctor," I told her. "I'll be there soon."

She agreed. That was the last time I ever heard her voice.

I was working a New York–Munich flight. It was routine.

Familiar. The layover in Munich was calm and pleasant. But on the morning of our return flight, just as the crew was assembling at the gate, something strange happened.

A uniformed flight attendant walked up with a woman in a business suit. She had that tight-lipped expression that told me something was off even before she opened her mouth.

"Which of you is Kirt VanBuren?" I

raised my hand, instantly alert.

"You will not be returning to New York today," she said. "You've been replaced on this flight. Please follow me to my office."

The words spun in my head. What the hell was happening?

In her office, she handed me a phone and told me to call Crew Scheduling. Now, let me explain something. Crew Scheduling is the nerve center of a flight attendant's life. They control everything: your flights, your off days, your fate.

They were the gatekeepers of news, both routine and life-altering. If someone back home had an emergency, they were the ones who took the call. It was not easy to get a message through. The caller had to go through reservations, confirm their relationship to you, provide your birthdate, mailing address, and everything.

Only then would Crew Scheduling intervene.

I dialed the number with shaking hands. A scheduler picked up.

"What's your employee ID?" he asked. Hesitantly, I gave it to him.

"Name of your next of kin?"

"My mother."

"Her name and address?"

I answered each question as calmly as I could, even though my heart was slamming against my ribs. Then came the silence followed by the sound of his keyboard clicking.

Finally, he said, "Your mother called. It's about your grandmother."

I froze. I didn't even breathe.

"We've cleared all upcoming flights from your schedule. Pan Am has booked you a seat on the KLM flight from Munich non-stop to Jamaica. You'll leave tonight. First class. The station manager will handle the ticketing details."

He paused, then said, almost like a machine, "Safe travels."

Then the line went dead.

35

"No Grandma, Please Don't Go!"

I STOOD THERE, DAZED, STARING AT THE phone like it might speak again. I wanted to scream. I wanted answers. I wanted to call Jamaica collect and talk to someone, anyone, but the station manager pushed a printed ticket into my hand and told me I had under two hours before the KLM flight departed. It was 6:20 p.m.

The flight was at 8:00. The terminal felt surreal. My Pan Am uniform felt tight, like a second skin I couldn't wait to shed. First class on the flight meant nothing to me. I sat there, surrounded by fine China and crystal glasses, staring straight ahead. I didn't eat. I didn't drink. I didn't even close my eyes.

Eight long and torturous hours with no information killed me inside. The hum of the plane and the sound of my thoughts screamed louder than the engines. What had happened? Was she in the hospital? Was she still alive? Or... had I missed my chance to say goodbye?

As soon as I cleared customs at Norman Manley International Airport, I didn't pause. I didn't look around. I didn't breathe. I headed straight for the row of pay phones. My heart hammered like it was trying to escape.

I called my mother collect. She picked up almost immediately. "Where are you?"

"I'm at the airport, Mom."

"Take a taxi straight to Kingston Public Hospital. Ward 30, Critical Care. Ask for Nurse Jackson. She's waiting for you. Don't stop anywhere. Just go." I didn't ask a single question. I didn't need to. I could feel it in my bones. Something was terribly wrong.

Outside, a sea of taxi drivers buzzed around me like bees to honey. "Who can get me to Kingston Public fast?" I shouted.

Every hand shot up. One man grabbed my flight bag and started walking. He was my ride. The thirty minute drive from the airport felt like it stretched across an eternity. I sat rigid in the back seat of that cab in my Pan Am uniform, staring blankly out the window while my mind spiraled. My grandmother (the woman who raised me and protected me) was in the hospital.

And no one could tell me what the hell was going on.

I handed the driver a crisp U.S. bill when we arrived. He beamed, but I didn't care. I was already scanning for the entrance to Ward 30.

36
Saying Goodbye to Grandma

A SECURITY GUARD SPOTTED ME. HE TOOK one look at my uniform and assumed I was American military. I didn't correct him. I didn't have time. "Ward 30. Critical Care." He took me there himself. Inside, the air was too cold. My flight bags hit the floor at the nurses' station. An older woman looked up. "Mr. Anderson...Oh my! You look just like your picture. Your grandmother raved about you. She's been showing everyone your flight attendant graduation photo. She couldn't wait to come visit you."

With a soft voice, I told nurse Jackson about my last conversation with grandma. "She told me she was having a little pain in her stomach. What happened?"

The light dimmed in nurse Jackson's eyes. "Your grandmother was in far more pain than she let on. The doctor ran some tests, and when they came back strangely abnormal, he decided to open her up. But as soon as he did, he saw it: gangrene. It had already taken over her abdomen. He made a larger cut, and... it was everywhere. There was nothing he could do but stitch her back up." I staggered back like she had physically struck me.

"She went into a coma this morning," she continued. "That's when we called your mother, but your grandmother had already asked for you. She wanted you here."

"Can I see her?"

She led me down the hallway. I braced myself with every step. There, tucked in the corner of the ward, was the woman who had given me the love my parents never did. Tubes snaked from her frail body. Machines hissed. I stood still, breath frozen in my throat. "Talk to her," she whispered. "She can hear you."

I took grandma's hand. It felt like paper. "Grandma... it's me, Kirt. I came as fast as I could. I was in Germany."

Immediately, the heart monitor spiked.

"What's going on?" I gasped.

"That's her way of telling you she hears you," the nurse said. "She's excited. Keep talking to her."

I sat beside her and let the rage boil over into grief.

"Why didn't you tell me how bad it was? You know I would've been here in a heartbeat. You didn't have to face this alone. You didn't have to pretend to be strong for me. I still need you..."

37

She's Gone, But Kill The Motherfucker

I LOOKED AT HER BEDSIDE TABLE AND SAW a shrine to our bond: her hairbrush, her red lipstick, her powder puff. And there it was: my flight attendant graduation photo, proudly framed beside a metal bedpan. I stayed with her through the night. By morning, I was hollow. Nurse Jackson took me to the employee cafeteria. She got me a cup of coffee, a croissant, and a donut. I laid my head down in the cafeteria and dozed off.

When I opened my eyes, it was 11:30. I ran back to Ward 30. The door was locked. I banged on it. No answer. I sprinted around to the window and what I saw broke me.

Doctors and nurses surrounded her, frantically doing chest compressions. I screamed.

I banged on the glass. "That's my grandmother! *Let me in!*"

And then... they stopped. One doctor looked up and met my eyes. Through the glass, he mouthed: I'm sorry."

I collapsed, but the pain wasn't done with me yet. I made a call to the house, needing something, anything, to tether me.

Cleon, the gardener, answered. "Mr. Kirt? Where are you? Do you know what's happening with your grandmother?"

"I arrived last night Cleon, and went straight to the hospital. I did see her. She's gone. It happened about an hour ago. I am still at the hospital."

He fell silent. Then, slowly, he said, "She was supposed to go to the doctor that day you told her to. She asked your father to take her. And you know what he said? He said he didn't have time to waste with her and told her to call a cab."

"What?" I snapped.

"I swear, sir. And then I saw him later that same day—down at the bar drinking with his buddies."

I couldn't listen to another word. "I've heard enough Cleon. Thanks for letting me know."

"He's on his way to the hospital now, Mr. Kirt, but I don't think he knows that she died."

I hung up. I started packing her things. Her lipstick. The photo. The powder puff. Every item felt sacred now.

About 35 minutes later, he stumbled in—half drunk.

The first thing out of his mouth: "So, the old lady's gone huh." No "hello," no "how are you," nothing. The rage in me hit the boiling point.

"You told her to go take a taxi to the doctor while you sat in a bar getting drunk?" I snarled.

"You're a fucking disgrace."

"And you're a piece of shit!"

He staggered toward me. I didn't hesitate.

I picked up the metal bedpan and slammed it across his face. Blood gushed from his face and soaked in the collar of his shirt. "You better not come anywhere near me, or I will kill you!"

The nurses heard the commotion and rushed in, chaos exploded.

"He hit me with the bedpan!" he slurred. "Call the police. I am pressing charges!"

"It should have been you in that bed, not her!" I screamed with rage. I felt like a bull ready to lunge at him.

The head nurse stepped between us. "Enough! Let her die in peace. She can still hear you. The brain is the last organ to go."

We were both breathing heavy. But then she turned to him with steel in her voice.

"Mr. Anderson... you'll have to leave. Ms. Mason loved her grandson. She never mentioned you. Not once. And I've never seen you visit her. I'm afraid I must ask you to go."

We stared at each other—him, with hatred; me, still holding the bed pan. My stare was far deeper.

It was a look of disgust.

38

The Last Bag She Carried

THE ROOM HAD GONE STILL. THE MACHINES were silent, the nurses were gone, and my father, bloodied and humiliated, had long since disappeared. It was just me now. Me and her.

I began to gather her things, folding each item with the reverence of a ritual.

Her   slippers.

Her head scarf.

A newspaper from two days ago, creased in the corner where she had started a crossword puzzle, she'd never finish.

And then, sitting quietly at the foot of her bed, was the bag. That bag.

The one I'd given her when I graduated Pan Am in 1982. It was navy blue with gold trim.

The wings were still proudly embroidered on the side. She had brought it with her to the hospital.

Of all things, that's what she used to pack her stuff.

It made me smile through the ache in my chest. That bag had seen the world, just like me. And now it had made its final journey back to her.

I don't know what came over me at that moment. Maybe it was curiosity. Maybe it was madness. Maybe it was love reaching for something one last time. But I leaned in and gently opened her left eyelid.

Her eyes were blue. Startling, vibrant, impossibly blue. I jerked back in disbelief. My grandmother had been born with soft grey eyes, pale like early morning fog.

This wasn't that. This was something otherworldly. I closed her eyelids quickly, almost like I had seen something I wasn't supposed to.

That image would never leave me. Not in this life.

Two attendants came in then.

They were quiet, respectful, and detached in the way that only those who deal with death daily can be.

They transferred her body to the gurney with care.

I gave them one clear instruction...

"Take her to Madden's Funeral Home. Nowhere else. And here, give them this business card."

All Pan Am flight attendants were issued business cards. It

was standard procedure.

They nodded. No questions asked.

I stood by the door as they wheeled her away. Her body was draped in a white sheet.

Her presence still somehow filled the room behind them.

My tears came, slow and steady.

They carved quiet trails down my cheeks. But I didn't wipe them away.

I let them fall. And they fell hard. I was broken and torn.

Still, there was no time to fall apart.

I had a funeral to plan, as much as it greatly pained me. And I wasn't going to let her go like just anybody.

She had raised me. Sheltered me. Fed me.

Protected me.

Fought for me.

She deserved a sendoff fit for a royal Queen. Two weeks. That's what I gave myself.

Two weeks to plan a farewell that would make the angels stop and take notice.

What I didn't know then (what no one could have warned me about) was that in those two weeks, the mask of mourning would slip from more than a few faces.

Secrets would rise like smoke.

Hidden enemies would emerge.

And the funeral that was meant to honor her would nearly destroy me.

39

The Funeral, The Will, The Graveside

DISORIENTED, I SLOWLY WALKED OUT OF the hospital. The weight of finality pressed down on me until I burst into tears. My grandma was gone! For real. And though my eyes were swollen from the tears, my mind had already shifted into battle mode.

There was no time for mourning. Not yet. Getting myself together, I had a funeral to plan. And I was going to send her off like a queen.

Numb inside, I drove straight to her house, pushed open the front door, and the dead silence knocked the wind out of me. Audibly, I gasped. Her spirit still lingered, but the warmth was gone. Just stillness. I sat in her bedroom and looked around, trying to figure out where the hell to begin.

First call: Nolan Bramwell. He was my ride-or-die since Jamaica College. We had been through it all. We used to sneak into nightclubs and party, we used to shoplift together, we used to swap stories about the same guys, and we kept secrets so dark we never whispered them out loud. He was now a high-profile lawyer.

Grandma adored him, even when she scolded me that he was "trouble wrapped in charm."

When I told him that she died, he heard the grief in my voice, and before I could say another word, he whispered, "I'm on my way."

And just like that, I had backup.

⚘

Thankfully, Nolan arrived an hour later, and the moment I saw him, I broke apart at the seams. I cried harder than I did in the hospital. He held me like only someone who truly knew me, could, then we pulled ourselves together and got down to business.

We needed documents. Insurance policies. Bank records. Her will. Anything that would help make sense of the madness she left behind. But Grandma's version of "filing" was chaos.

Papers were inside coat pockets, folded between bed linens, even stuffed inside old handbags.

It was an archaeological dig with no map or directions.

We cataloged every bank, every insurance company, every name we could find.

But still, there was no Will.

I started making appointments. The lawyers were surprisingly cooperative. They told me nothing could move forward without certified death certificates—at least six copies.

Since Grandma had an account with them, they took care of the paperwork for me. I handed over my U.S. passport, filled out some forms, and then came the first bright spot.

I was listed as the beneficiary on two of her stock accounts.

That gave me a little breathing room. Screw that, I was relieved.

Next, it was time to head to Maddens Funeral Home. I had to see caskets and find a church. But right off the bat, they told me Jamaica was facing a flower shortage.

Roses and tulips, my grandma's favorites, were in short supply. And the caskets? Absolutely not. Nothing elegant. Nothing fitting for a woman of her class.

Good thing I worked for an airline.

I flew to Miami the next day on the early morning flight, found a stunning lilac casket lined in a soft purple satin and arranged for one-hundred dozen roses and tulips to be flown in. I returned on the late flight Miami back to Kingston.

Thanks to Pan Am, cargo space was free. I told Maddens they'd only be responsible for embalming, dressing the body, and printing the programs. And I meant what I said.

Now I just needed to find a final resting place.

DOVECOT FUNERAL PARK HAD JUST OPENED months earlier. They offered me a plot beneath a large, gorgeous hibiscus tree. I didn't hesitate. I bought two plots: one for her and one for myself. But of course, nothing came easy.

The grave diggers were on strike. It was their fourth week of being off the job. Their labor union and management had failed to reach an equitable agreement.

I begged for the union leader's phone number. When we met, he poured out his frustration. They were treated poorly, they were disrespected and taken for granted.

I pulled out my Pan Am union card, with the International Brotherhood of Teamsters (IBT), and showed him. I let him know that I understood what it meant to fight for dignity, and I, too, was part of a strike once where the airline pilots and flight attendants walked a picket line.

"She's not just anyone," I said to him. "She raised me. This isn't just a burial. It's a legacy."

I told him the story about her coming to visit and how much preparation I had done before she arrived. Memories, memories, memories! You'd swear it was the arrival of the Queen of England. I didn't realize I was in tears, but he understood.

We walked the cemetery together. I
showed him the double plot. "This
one's hers. This one's mine."

For a long, drawn out moment he looked at me. Then he nodded and said. "Four men. One day's work. USD $250 each. And a couple bottles of that 120 overproof Jamaican white rum."

Deal.

Nolan never left my side. Day five, we were still moving. Day six, the lawyers called. The death certificates were ready, and the letters for the banks were prepared.

Thank God! He got all the glory!

First, we went to the bank. Unsurprisingly, the manager was kind. She said that Grandma always talked about her "beloved grandson who flies for Pan Am."

Bittersweetly, I smiled, holding back tears.

After verifying my passport, Pan Am ID, and Social Security card, she said, "You want to close the account or keep it open?" Then came the twist. "Oh—and there's her safety deposit box."

Nolan and I looked at each other with non-verbal communication, like *WTF!*

What. The. Fuck!

In shock, we followed her to the vault. My breathing increased every step that we took. My hands were clammy and itching.

Inside were grandma's stocks, bonds, a few pieces of glittering diamond jewelry, and a plain envelope.

I opened it and looked at Nolan.

There it was.

Grandma's Last Will and Testament.

40
Grandma's Last Will and Testament

I NEARLY DROPPED IT. NOLAN AND I LOCKED eyes, but when we read it... silence. My stomach dropped. It was incomplete.

The witness signatures, my mother and my cousin, were there. The trustees were listed as my Aunt Amy, one of grandma's cousins and her youngest brother, but the body of the Will...

Empty.

No instructions.

No division of assets.

Just... blank.

We sat in the car, staring at the Will like it might magically fill itself in. Finally, Nolan said what we were both thinking: "Let's finish what she started."

He dug out his old typewriter, and together we

reconstructed what she should have written. Everything she had back then in 1974, the year listed on the Will, we started deciding what we would give to my father.

The old Vauxhall Viva car, the three properties she no longer owned. It was a neat distraction.

Then we got real.

The remaining assets, the house in Jamaica, the ones in London and the USA, the stocks, the accounts (everything still current) went to me, her only grandson.

And to soothe my conscience, I added a clause: my father could live in the house until his death or, if we both agreed to sell, he'd get one-third. I'd take the remaining two-thirds.

We gave the completed Will to the lawyers. We told them we found it in the safety deposit box.

Case closed.

And for every nosy, greedy relative circling like vultures, I had copies ready and waiting. The reaction was delicious. They were livid. Furious. But powerless.

The funeral day came heavy with heat and secrets. I had told my mother to take my suit to the church, and I would meet her there.

Meanwhile, I was at the funeral home watching my loving

grandmother being prepared to be put into the casket.

Miss Dorette, the make-up artist, had been doing this for over forty years, she boasted, but this time I was in charge.

I wanted grandma to be holding a white bible in one hand and a red rose in the other. This meant breaking her arms which were frozen, so they told me to look away. I cringed inside, but time wasn't on my side.

As Ms. Dorette was stuffing cotton in her jaw to pump up her cheeks, I pulled out a makeup kit. "I have my own makeup she said."

I glared at her. "Well, you won't be using it today. You will be using what I brought."

Oooooh, she was extremely pissed! Immediately, she stormed off to get her supervisor, as if that was going to change anything. I said what I said, when I said it, and how I said it. Period, with a side of point blank range and a bulls-eye on the rocks, bitch. Of course, she had to end up using my makeup. The owner, Mr. Madden, explained that grandma needed a heavy foundation because of the body being thawed out too quickly from the heat.

Mind you, the ceremony was four hours long. So, understanding that, I compromised.

The casket would be open for about three to four hours

until it was sealed before heading to the funeral plot.

I arrived with the hearse and ran to a room in the back of the church to change.

As the casket was being positioned by the altar with the pallbearers, I was changing in the vestibule, when I noticed the box of programs. I picked it up and I emerged.

I called a few of my cousins over to hand out the programs. Everyone was watching me. They were waiting to see what kind of send-off I'd give her. And it was flawless. The flowers, the casket, and the music was her royal farewell.

When I was drafting the funeral program, I found Grandma's passport renewal picture. It was a beautiful photo.

I remembered four hymns that she liked.

I asked the Pastor if his musical director was familiar with them and he said yes.

I asked a few of my relatives to do remembrances, as you knew her speeches for the slow people in the back, and slotted myself to say a few words.

Don't ask me why I did that because I myself couldn't answer that question.

The church was packed. There was about two-hundred people in attendance.

After a few people sauntered by, I took my seat on the front pew. I sat at the furthest end just so I didn't have to be near my father. I was between Mummy and Nolan.

Many people came up to me to give their condolences and said how beautiful she looked in the casket.

All I could do was nod in acknowledgment. I didn't speak. Everything was going great until it was my time to speak. I pre-wrote my speech so it wouldn't take a long time. The casket was still open.

I adjusted the microphone and started speaking. "Hello, everyone. Thank you all for coming out to say farewell to my grandmother."

I looked down at the open casket and I couldn't say anything. Everyone was quiet. I tried to say something else, but it got worse. For every word I spoke, my voice cracked, and the tears flowed. Finally, Nolan came on stage and held me. He took me back to my seat.

The hush in the church was deafening.

Nolan finished the speech and thanked everyone again and then the Minister took over and concluded the program. As he gave the benediction, I got up in the middle of it and walked out of the church.

I didn't look at anyone. I headed to my mother's car. I wasn't in the mood to talk to anyone.

I just wanted to be left alone.

⸻❧⸻

After the ceremony concluded, we headed to the Dovecot graveyard. The gravediggers did a beautiful job, and all four men were there to make sure everything was okay. As the minister did the verse "ashes to ashes, dust to dust," a few people threw flowers and some gravel on the lowered casket.

Then my father stepped up to the edge of the grave, pretending to mourn. I stood behind him, staring down at the casket. My hands were clenched. Just one nudge, one little push and he would be right in the grave with her...

But as my hand went up, someone yanked my jacket.

It was my cousin Frank. He was in the US Armed Forces and flew down for the funeral. He was the last child of my Aunt Rosemarie, the eleventh child.

He whispered in my ear: "Not today, Kirt. I heard what happened at the hospital."

41

Kiss My Ass, Fuck You, and Go To Hell

I NEVER WANTED TO SET FOOT AT THAT REPAST. Every fiber of my being screamed "Don't go." I had just buried the only person who had ever loved me without conditions, and now, somehow, I was expected to go sit with the mongrels and scavengers who spent years bleeding her dry.

But my mother, ever the polished diplomat, insisted. "Kirt, it would be rude if you didn't go," she said in that tone she used when she expected no argument. "You need to thank everyone for coming."

Against my better judgment, I gave in, but the pit in my stomach knew better. Something ugly was waiting for me and I was ready for battle.

Aunt Rosemarie, Grandma's only sister, who had eleven children. My father lived with her most of youthful life. He essentially became her twelfth child.

Some of them I didn't recognize, but the moment I stepped

through the front door, the air became thicker, hotter, and slimier.

Conversations fell to harsh whispers. Heads turned.

Eyes raked over me, sizing me up like a hawk who just spotted a bleeding rabbit. I offered a few stiff hellos and forced a smile, then I caught sight of my father cradling a drink in a corner, with his cousins consoling him. I immediately moved to the opposite side of the room.

I picked a chair in a far corner where they could all see me, and I could see every one of them. I didn't belong here.

And they knew it. My mother tried her best to play the role, when she didn't even know the part. Politely, she chatted with everyone. The consummate diplomat, even during extreme loss.

Yes, she lost a mother. My mother and grandmother were extremely close even after the divorce and my grandmother would always say "Norma is the daughter I never had."

I silently pleaded for her to look over and rescue me.

Ten minutes ticked by. And then the eye of the storm came straight for me. My Aunt Rosemarie, Grandma's sister with the eleven children who my father grew up with.

Aunt Rosemarie had always been a hurricane in human form. Mean as a snake, and twice as venomous.

She carved through the crowd without pretending to be

gracious. Her face was hard and pinched with contempt.

No condolences. No pretense.

She marched straight up to me, nostrils flaring.

Here we go, I thought.

"I can't believe my sister left everything to you and nothing to your father," she spat, loud enough for nearby eavesdroppers to catch every syllable. "You stole your father's birthright."

The room fell into an uncomfortable hush.

I smiled. It was a slow, cold, and sarcastic smile that didn't reach my eyes. I tilted my head, letting the silence hang for a moment just to make her squirm.

"Wherever you got your information from," I said, my voice dripping with syrupy sarcasm, "they should've told you that the will was made back in 1974. It was never updated to reflect the sales of the old properties, the car, or any of her other assets."

"Oh."

"So, mind your own god*damn* business. And stay out of mine." I said it as loud as I could so even the next door neighbors could hear it.

Of course, none of them knew the truth. There was no car, no real estate, no treasure chest left to find.

The real Will would have crushed any fantasy they were

clinging to. I had forged a softer version, a fairy tale for my father, so he wouldn't have to face the cold, hard truth.

But Aunt Rosemarie didn't care about facts. She wasn't looking for the truth. She was looking for a fight.

She jabbed her crooked, bony finger right into my face and sneered: "You better make sure you take care of your father financially."

Oh, no honey. Bitch! She said the wrong thing and made the wrong move. Slowly, I stood up, towering over her. The chair screeched across the tile. Yes, it was a warning shot.

"Oh, please," I said, my voice low and lethal. "Why don't you and your eleven children take care of him? After all, my grandmother, the woman you're pretending to mourn, paid for most of your children's educations."

"I'm tired of your smart mouth, Kirt."

"*Then go take a nap!*" I snapped. "Grandma kept your lights on when you couldn't. Put food on your table when you were too damn lazy to do it yourselves."

A few people gasped. Good. Let them.

42

Broken Wings

I TOOK A DELIBERATE STEP CLOSER, SMILING sweetly, but my words were battery acid thrown in a bitch's face.

"And you have the nerve, the audacity, to come at me with your finger wagging, like you're some moral authority? Honey, you better sit your ass down. I suggest that since most of you live in the USA, you can setup an account with a Jamaican bank and send him a monthly allowance."

Aunt Rosemarie's face turned an alarming shade of purple, but I wasn't finished. Not by a long shot.

"Let me be very clear: my grandmother didn't *like* you, your own sister despised you, Aunt Rosemarie. She said that you are a parasite and an ungrateful bitch!"

She clutched her pearls with her head tucked back.

"She spent her whole life trying to outgrow the swamp she was born in, and you are the last, rotting piece of it."

Gasps echoed around the room now. All conversation stopped. Everyone was watching. I took a breath, then continued.

"Now, you want to play family feud." My voice was sharper than a soprano doing her grand finale. "It's too late. Take that piece of trash over there, who calls himself my father, as well as your army of moochers, and go babysit my grandmother's son yourselves.

"And as far as I'm concerned, bitch," I continued, "you, him, and your entire sorry-ass clan can kiss my black ass and rot in hell. He will never see a penny of my grandmother's hard earned money." It was nuclear.

"You think she didn't know he would drink her hard earned money away. My grandmother was smarter than that. She knew what she was doing."

No coming back from it.

The room cracked wide open. People were shouting. Someone knocked over a plate of food.

I turned to my mother, who stood frozen in horror, and said loud enough for everyone to hear: "Mummy, I *told* you I didn't want to come around these vultures. Especially her sister, the despicable bitch who may soon drop dead herself! *Goodbye*, rodent!"

Then, without another word, I grabbed my mother's hand and marched us out of the door.

I slammed it behind me with a force that rattled the whole damn house. *Bitch*! Outside, the air was thick, but it smelled like rain, salt, and freedom. I took a deep breath. My heart was hammering and pounding against my ribs.

It's over. It's finally over. No more pretending. No more playing nice with people who would've gutted me if they thought there was a dollar to be made. I fought for my grandmother in life, and I fought for her in death. Now it was time to finish the business, settle the estate, and get the hell back home to the USA.

Where I belong.

I never spoke to any of the family again.

Returning to New York after my grandmother's funeral I felt like stepping back into a world that hadn't paused to grieve with me. Everything moved at its usual pace, but inside me, everything had stopped. I was hollow.

The woman who had raised me, the woman who protected me from truths too heavy for a child to carry, was gone. My foundation, my fortress, was gone. I had flown thousands of miles in my career, but this time, I was barely holding altitude.

I got a call from my manager the next day asking how I was feeling. I said I was fine and that I wanted to return to work. I figured that throwing myself back to flying would help me forget about what happened in Jamaica.

The next day I got a call from Pan Am operations saying that I had a flight to Paris the next day. I reported for duty like clockwork, slipping on my Pan Am uniform, my second skin.

It was pressed to perfection. Every button was closed, and my shoes were polished. Deep inside, I was unraveling.

I boarded the Paris-bound flight. My face was calmness. My grief was tucked tightly under layers of professionalism.

Until it wasn't.

Midway through the flight, first class was quiet. There were soft conversations, clinking silverware, and the hush of privilege in motion. I carried a silver tray of six champagne flutes, filled to the rim, balancing it easily in one hand as I had done hundreds of times before.

I smiled politely as I approached a couple in 2A and 2C, but then, something cracked.

Maybe it was the way the woman smiled, a sound that echoed something familiar. Maybe it was the glint of a wedding ring that reminded me of my grandmother's hands, always adorned with jewelry.

Or maybe it was just the emptiness of knowing she would never see me polished, poised, pretending.

The tray slipped.

It didn't tumble; it crashed.

All six flutes shattered in front of all the passengers: champagne spraying like broken dreams.

Gasps erupted through first class. I stood frozen, staring at the wreckage as if it were a body. My body. My grief. My shattered world.

Without thinking, I dropped to my knees, hands reaching for the glass shards. And that's when it happened.

The hot and blinding tears streamed down my face without warning or permission. I was sobbing. Gut-deep, broken sobs. In front of the crème de la crème of Pan Am's elite passengers.

Two gentlemen rose from their seats, rushing toward me.

"Careful," one said gently, taking my wrist as I reached for a jagged edge. The other helped sweep aside the napkins soaked in champagne. I couldn't speak. I was choking on air, on sorrow, on humiliation.

The noise had drawn the Flight Leader's attention. Her name was Monica. She came running from the upper galley, heels clicking urgently against the floor. Her eyes scanned the scene.

When she saw me on my knees, tear-streaked, with passengers stooped to help, she didn't ask a single question.

She knelt beside me, placed a firm hand on my shoulder, and calmly addressed the cabin. "Ladies and gentlemen, thank you for your kindness. If I could kindly ask you to return to your seats. We've got it from here."

The passengers obeyed.

43

Meeting Enid

A *FEW OF THE PASSENGERS GAVE QUIET NODS* of sympathy as they returned to their champagne, caviar and foie gras, perhaps recognizing that they had just witnessed a rare kind of turbulence.

The Flight Leader leaned closer, her voice lowered. "Go take a break," she said. "I've got this. I know what this is about."

I didn't argue. I couldn't. My face said everything. The passengers knew something was wrong and I think she told them afterwards that I had just buried my grandmother.

I stumbled into the crew rest area on the 747 aircraft, ripped off my tie, and let the sobs come until I couldn't breathe.

I couldn't finish the flight. I didn't speak as we headed to our layover hotel.

I sat at the back of the van. I don't think my coworkers knew what to say, so they left me alone.

In my hotel room I had some Bacardi rum, Johnny Walker whiskey and some Bombay Sapphire gin. I started binge drinking each little miniature bottle, then my hotel room phone rang.

It was my manager. He was alerted to what had happened. He told me that I would be replaced for the return trip and that I was to come and see him once I arrived back at the base.

I sat during the return flight.

I was deadheaded, a term used when a crew member was not working but being positioned to start a trip somewhere other than their base.

As I approached my manager's office, I was fully expecting to be grounded from flying.

Instead, he gently closed the door, slid a paper across the desk, and said, "Take two weeks off. You are officially on a compassionate leave of absence, and I want you to call this number. It's someone that you can talk to. You have to be cleared by a psychologist before you return to duty."

I learned that sometimes, even the strongest wings need time to mend.

I called everyone to let them know about Grandma's passing. I was going through my rolodex and came upon Enid's name. I contemplated calling.

I mean she did know my grandmother.

Without further ado, I hesitantly dialed the number.

It rang twice before a young, vibrant voice answered.

"Hello?"

"Hi, um... may I speak with Enid?"

"She's at work right now, but I'm her daughter."

"Um, okay..."

"Can I take a message?"

Something tightened in my chest. Her daughter. I paused.

For a moment, I considered hanging up. But my voice betrayed my thoughts.

"Could you just let her know Kirt Anderson called .....you know what, never mind, I'll just call back." I said.

There was a beat of silence.

Then came the question that would shift the ground beneath me.

"Wait a minute ....are you my brother, Kirt?"

The word *brother* sounded like it didn't belong to me. Yet somehow, it did.

"I... I guess I am."

She erupted into excitement, as if she'd been waiting her whole life for that moment.

She said her name was Donna and that she was my big sister.

She stated that she'd always known she had a brother out there. Enid had told them. She wanted to know everything.

Where I lived, what I did, how Paris had been, how I ended up in New York.

It was a tidal wave of curiosity crashing into a man still learning how to swim in his own story.

I downplayed it all. "I'm in New York now. I'm working as a flight attendant for Pan Am."

I kept it light and detached.

But Donna wasn't letting go that easy.

"Well, when are you coming to Fort Lauderdale? You have to meet everyone!"

I tried to sidestep it. "I'll speak with Enid and let her decide."

But she was already launching into family introductions. She said I had two other sisters, Sandree and Michelle, who was the last sister. She had a baby named Lloyd when she was fifteen.

Donna said she and Lloyd shared the same birthday in November. She also mentioned that she had just earned a track scholarship to Louisiana State University in Baton Rouge and was set to leave soon.

I smiled politely on the phone, mentally trying to exit the

conversation.

Before hanging up, she added, almost casually, "Mom's been working for the District Attorney's office for over twenty-five years since she left the airlines. She'll be so thrilled that you called. I'll get word to her now."

Five minutes later, my phone rang. It was Enid.

Her voice was breathless with emotion.

"Kirt?" she said my name like a prayer. "I've waited so long to hear your voice."

It took a moment for me to say anything. "I have something to tell you...my grandmother died."

I fell silent. Curiosity beat out fear, and I agreed to meet her at the end of the month.

As the date approached, doubt crept in.

What was I doing?

Did I really want to face this family who I'd never known?

But something (maybe guilt, maybe curiosity) pushed me forward.

Inevitably, I flew to Ft. Lauderdale. My mind was racing a mile a second.

Donna picked me up from the airport like I was a soldier

returning from war.

She wrapped her arms around me, holding on like she might lose me again.

Then she stepped back and stared, like I was an artifact in a museum, something rare and maybe too delicate to touch.

When Donna met me at the airport, she explained that Enid had been called away on a last-minute business trip and wouldn't be there.

I exhaled quietly, grateful for the reprieve; for now, I would only be meeting the other two sisters, Michelle and Sandree, and that felt like all I could handle.

Immediately, Michelle and I clicked. I didn't like Sandree

44

Closer to One, Lost to Another

MICHELLE AND I BEGAN SPEAKING REGULARLY. Her voice became familiar, grounding. Unlike Donna's enthusiasm or Enid's maternal insistence, Michelle spoke with clarity, patience, and a quiet intuition that always seemed to know when I needed silence more than answers.

She never pushed or pried. She offered herself as someone willing to listen. Slowly, I opened up. I told her about Paris. I talked about Pan Am. I also told her about the surreal feeling of stepping into a family I'd never known and wanting to step back out.

She didn't judge me. She simply said, "I figured as much. You've been your own person for a long time. It's hard to rewire that overnight."

There was something reassuring about her. She didn't ask for brotherly bonding, and she didn't talk like someone trying to make up for lost time.

She understood distance and respected it.

One evening, she called. I remember the tone in her voice. Different. Tight. Sad. "Kirt... I have to tell you something."

My heart dropped. I don't know why, but I knew it wasn't good. She was sobbing.

"It's Donna," she admitted. I sat down, gripped the arm of my chair. "She's dead."

The silence on my end was heavy. Paralyzing. "Dead? How? When?" I finally whispered.

Michelle took a shaky breath. "Her boyfriend... Lucky. The one she was trying to leave. He bought her a car for Christmas, but he tampered with the brakes. She didn't know. She drove it. The crash was... bad."

I was frozen in time. My mind reeled back to the moment Donna had wrapped her arms around me at the airport. Her eyes were full of light, a thousand questions, and dreams she hadn't even lived yet.

I remembered her telling me about that track scholarship. Baton Rouge. The future. Her future.

Michelle continued. "She knew he was dangerous, Kirt. He was jealous, controlling... a drug dealer with a violent streak. She was trying to get out. That scholarship was her way out."

I didn't speak. I couldn't. It was the kind of loss that didn't come with tears at first, but lead with shock and a sickening sense of unreality.

"He's under investigation," Michelle said, her voice shaking now. "Everyone knows he did it. But proving it..."

She didn't finish. She didn't need to.

I sat there in the quiet aftermath, thinking about all the what-ifs. What if I had stayed longer?

What if I had gotten to know her better?

What if I had warned her, guided her, protected her?

But what-ifs don't change the ending.

Donna had embraced me like a brother from the very first second, while I was still trying to convince myself I was one. And now she was gone. Just like that.

I kept in touch with Michelle more after that. It wasn't out of guilt. It was something deepening. We were two people shaped by silence, secrets, and survival. Two people who didn't need to pretend, because we'd already lived the truth.

No, I didn't go to the funeral. I couldn't. I told Michelle I was traveling overseas. She didn't press. Maybe she understood. Maybe she didn't.

But that night, I poured myself a drink, sat by the window

in my New York apartment, and listened to Donna's voice on my old voicemail.

Just one more time. It was bright. Hopeful. Full of the future. She would never run that race at The Louisiana State University in Baton Rouge.

But I could still hear her voice like it was yesterday.

"Wait a minute... are you my brother, Kirt?"

45

My Sister, The Crook

ENID NEVER RECOVERED. NOT REALLY. THE DAY Donna died, a part of her spirit left with her. That boundless energy I heard when she first called me vanished overnight. It was Michelle who told me what happened the night the police came to the door. They didn't say much. They didn't have to.

They came holding a Ziploc evidence bag containing Donna's driver's license, her gold nameplate necklace, and the watch she wore every day, the one Lucky had given her for her birthday.

Enid collapsed.

Right there in the doorway, she folded in on herself like her entire soul had crumbled. She was inconsolable, barely breathing, as if some instinct inside her had shut everything down to protect her from a truth too unbearable to hold.

From that day on, Enid's home became quieter. Dimmer. She wore her pain like bone marrow to it recipient.

She was never too far from breaking. Donna had been her eldest child and her bright star. The one who had wrapped me in that fierce, breathless hug when I first stepped off the plane. The one who had believed in second chances and family reunions and my vulture family back in Jamaica could stay in hell.

Her death was never just an accident. Not to us.

Not to anyone who knew Lucky.

He was known on the streets as charming and generous when it served him, but behind closed doors, he was possessive, violent, and deeply unstable.

Donna had been trying to leave him. That scholarship to LSU was her ticket out, and he knew it. So, he bought her a car for Christmas, a sleek red coupe, shiny and brand new. Only it wasn't a gift.

It was a trap.

He tampered with the brakes, and no one found out until it was too late.

No charges were ever filed. Insufficient evidence, they said. But we knew. We all knew.

Lucky was later killed in a drug deal gone wrong. Karma is a bitch. After the funeral, whatever held the family together began to fray.

Without Donna, the balance was gone.

Secrets hidden beneath polite introductions and family cookouts unraveled fast. I later saw a copy of the funeral program. I was listed as her brother.

Many people were confused. "Brother? Did Donna have a brother? Where is he? How come we never knew that?"

Those were questions asked, but were never answered. That was when I started to see the real Enid family.

The version that didn't make it into holiday cards.

Michelle and I still spoke, but something in her started to shift. She'd once been the calm, wise voice that reached out with compassion. Now she spoke in half-coded language about "money moves" and "opportunities."

I didn't want to understand. Then when I visited her, she said "I have a surprise for you."

Before I left on my return flight that afternoon, she handed me a Discover credit card with my name on it.

I froze. "How did you even...?"

"It's a gift," she said casually. "You're an authorized user now. I won't be using it."

My blood ran cold. She said it like she'd just handed me a birthday cake.

I realized that Michelle was scheming to survive.

Deeply embedded in fraud, Michelle ran credit card scams for years. The family rumor mill said she'd served a four-year prison sentence for it, but no one dared talk too loud. About it.

She was smart, slick, and dangerously charming. She knew how to disappear in plain sight.

Sandree wasn't far behind. Enid's second oldest daughter, after me, had a smile like Donna's but a shadow behind her eyes. She was beautiful, unpredictable, and just as tangled in deception.

A warrant had been issued for her arrest years earlier for fraud again, but she was always one step ahead.

She knew how to keep moving, and how to dodge the system like she was born to.

And then there was Lloyd. Michelle's son. He was born when she was just fifteen on Donna's birthday. He'd grown up watching his mother outwit banks, skirt court summons, manipulate phone reps with fake identities, and coach others through scams like they invented it.

By the time he was sixteen, he had followed her into the life of fraud and scams.

But he didn't stop there.

Lloyd had built a network that stretched into federal

agencies and public offices.

He had someone at the DMV who could produce clean IDs, someone in the Department of Children and Families who could run background checks and forge documents, a FedEx contact for package logistics, and a postal worker to move fraudulent checks across state lines.

They printed checks.

Cashed them.

Bought goods.

Laundered cash.

It was sophisticated.

And for a while, it worked.

I watched all of it unfold like I was staring into a house I had no business being in.

I thought I had discovered a family.

What I had really stepped into was a slick, corrupted, and desperate machine and I wasn't about to be the WD-40.

They didn't see it that way. To

them, it was survival.

To me, it was betrayal.

Not every reunion was a gift.

Sometimes, it's a warning.

Sometimes the blood that binds you is the same blood that led to fingerprinting and mug shots.

And as much as Michelle tried to keep me close, I knew I was drifting away from the bullshit.

The same instinct that carried me from Jamaica to Paris, from Paris to New York, now screamed a word louder than the rest: Run!

Part 2

My Evolution

46

My Journey into the Skies

I've kissed men, and sometimes women, beneath neon dragons, raced across ancient stones in Prada loafers, and found midnight comfort in the arms of strangers who spoke no English but knew every part of me.

FOUR FLIGHT ATTENDANTS, FRESH OFF A thirteen-hour haul from JFK to Beijing, high on caffeine and duty-free Toblerone, dared each other to a sprint up the Great Wall of China.

We changed out of our uniforms, dragging ourselves to meet up in the hotel lobby where we hired a van to take us. We reached one of the seven wonders of the world.

We climbed up the crumbling, uneven stairs like some glamorous emergency drill, and I was wheezing like a broken tea kettle. But I couldn't stop laughing.

Neither could Lucas.

Lucas was an Australian flight attendant with a voice like velvet and shoulders that didn't quit. We'd flown together once before on a Paris rotation, but this layover was longer, looser, and more charged. We'd been messaging each other for days before the trip, trading photos, playlists, and not-so-subtle innuendos.

By the time we landed in Beijing, the chemistry between us was thick with our own private thoughts.

After our wall-top race and a hundred selfies later, we headed back to the hotel and peeled out of our sweat-soaked shirts.

We rode back to the hotel in silence. Our knees occasionally brushed together on the bumpy ride. At the hotel bar, he ordered us baijiu shots. It was China's version of rocket fuel, and by the third one, I was spilling secrets I hadn't said out loud in years. He leaned in. "I've waited three layovers for this." We kissed in the elevator.

ASIA WAS SEDUCTIVE IN WAYS THAT SNUCK up on me. In Bangkok, the humidity clung to my skin like a possessive lover. I'd met Jaywan on a travel app. He was a local university professor with a dimpled smile and a motorbike.

He took me to a night market where we ate noodles out of plastic bags and shared mango sticky rice under flickering neon lights. He didn't speak much English, but his hands were fluent.

We walked past temples with gold-roofed stupas glowing under the moonlight. At one point, he pulled me into a quiet alley, pressed his forehead to mine, and said something soft in Thai. I didn't need a translation. I felt it.

Tokyo was another kind of magic. I'd been obsessed with Japan since childhood. Samurai, cherry blossoms, anime, all of it. I didn't expect to find Haruki.

He was a bartender at a tucked-away speakeasy in Shibuya, a place you could only find if you knew someone who knew someone. His English was better than mine after three sakes.

He wore black like armor and had the kind of jawline that made you say stupid things.

We spent the night talking about books, Western movies, and how lonely it can be to always be "on." He walked me back to the crew hotel at 4 a.m., our fingers brushing occasionally, unsure of whether to grab hold or let go.

When I got to my room, he texted: "You are safe with me." I stared at that message until the sun came up.

HONG KONG, SEOUL, TAIPEI. *Each* city gave me something I didn't find anywhere else in the world. A flavor, a touch, a lesson. I began to realize that every layover wasn't just a break between flights, but it was also a new chance to be seen, touched, and understood, even if just for a few hours.

In Western cities, cautiously flirted, checking the temperature of a room. Yet in Asia, behind hotel room doors and blinking kanji signs, I found tenderness in the most unexpected places. And yet, it wasn't all perfect. There were moments of shame, of closeted hookups in anonymous rooms where we never said each other's names. Moments when I felt like a beautiful ghost, floating through those cities without roots, without consequences....

But then there were nights like the one in Shanghai, where a jazz pianist named Wei sang to me in Mandarin while I laid on his lap.

We were both wrapped in sheets and the moonlight. I didn't understand the lyrics, but I understood everything else.

There is a unique intimacy in fleeting encounters. They burn brighter. They scar deeper.

And, by the time my crew packed up for the next flight, I always left a piece of myself behind, whether it was on the stairs of the Great Wall, on the sweaty sheets of a Bangkok hostel, or in the quiet corners of a Tokyo bar.

Some men leave souvenirs. I

left memories.

47
Mile-High Masks

"The plane was my stage. I served caviar with a smile and heartbreak in my pocket. And somewhere between takeoff and turbulence, I became whoever the passenger needed me to be."

AT 35,000 FEET, THE AIR IS THINNER, THE truths are slipperier, and the lies, well, they glide like butter across a galley cart.

Flight attendants are shape-shifters. We're therapists in heels, bodyguards with cocktail shakers, undercover comedians, and silent witnesses to the wildest confessions never meant to land.

My mask was always perfect. Immaculate grooming. Colgate smile. Eyes kind, but unreadable. To the world, I was polished, poised, and oh-so-professional. But inside, I carried wounds older than my wings.

I remember when a groom cried in the jump seat beside me, thirty minutes before landing in Paris. He told me he wasn't ready. He'd just kissed his best man in the airport bathroom.

I told him to follow his heart. Then I served him champagne and a warm towel, like I hadn't just watched him unravel.

There was a soldier, home from Afghanistan, trembling so hard I held his hand.

He stared out the window and whispered, "I'm scared to touch my kids. What if they flinch?"

I put a blanket over his lap and tucked it in like he was my brother. He looked up at me and said, "You smell like safety."

There was a pastor in business class, traveling to a religious conference, who slipped me his hotel key scribbled with a Bible verse. I still remember what he said when I walked away: "Even angels get lonely."

But the hardest moment? It was mid-flight to Los Angeles, somewhere over Kansas, when I passed by the lavatory and caught my reflection in the mirror of the galley door.

I didn't recognize him. The man staring back had perfect posture, perfect diction, and perfect skin. However, there was a hollowness in his eyes. A vacancy. Like he'd been touched too often by people who never really saw him.

Like he'd given away pieces of himself in hotels, hammams, alleyways, and airport lounges, hoping to feel whole again.

That was the night I cried in my layover hotel room, curled up with my blanket and a pack of wet wipes. I didn't cry because I was ashamed. I cried because I couldn't tell where the act ended and I began.

But oh, we know how to bounce back.

The next flight, I pinched my cheeks, straightened my tie, and took a selfie with a movie star on her way to Tokyo. She called me "darling."

Can you imagine being called *darling* by Diahann Carroll. Her entourage asked for more hot towels. I flirted shamelessly with the closeted baseball player in 3A and got a wink in return.

Yes, that was my nickname for years   "Kirt The Flirt."

Sometimes validation came in the form of a compliment. Sometimes it came with room service and no strings. Sometimes it came from within, when I reminded myself that I wasn't just playing a part, but I was surviving.

What they didn't tell you when you joined this life was that the sky changed you. The altitude made your emotions volatile. You fell harder. Cried faster. Trust too easily. And when the plane landed, you walked off like none of it happened.

But it did.

Every whispered "thank you," every drunken confession

over gin and tonic, every stolen glance from a closeted executive... it stayed with you. It settled in your bones like jet fuel and lingered long after the passengers were gone.

And me?

I kept flying. Because the sky didn't judge me. The aircraft didn't care who I kissed. And somewhere between the lies I told at 38,000 feet and the truths I whispered into foreign pillows, I found fragments of the man I wanted to be.

Still broken. Still brilliant.

But finally... real.

48

Cockpit Confessions

"It wasn't just the passengers who were fascinating, it was the crew. The ones who drank their feelings at the hotel bar, loved fiercely behind closed doors, and treated every layover like their last.

IF THOSE GALLEYS COULD TALK, THEY'D RUIN marriages. If hotel hallways had eyes, they'd go blind. There's a myth that flight attendants only date pilots.

The truth?

We flirted with everyone. Pilots. Other flight attendants. Dispatchers. Sometimes, even the ground crew if the delay was long enough and the looks were worth it.

The attraction in the airline world wasn't always about looks. A knowing glance over coffee on Day 1 of a four-day trip. Shared snacks in the galley.

The casual "Where are you staying tonight?" that really means: Are we doing this or pretending again?

One of my first crew crushes was a male purser named Troy.

Former military, buzz cut, thighs like tree trunks, and a mouth that said "sir" like a prayer.

We worked a Tel Aviv turn together and barely spoke until the second leg.

After service, he leaned against the galley wall and said, "You're always this quiet, or are you just watching me?"

I smirked. "Would it make a difference?" He

smiled. "Room 819. After crew drinks."

I showed up. He didn't kiss me hello. He kissed me like he'd been waiting since takeoff.

Another time, on a Buenos Aires trip, I was paired with André. He was a Brazilian FA with green eyes and a silver tongue.

He walked with swagger and spoke like he knew every secret you were hiding.

We didn't even wait for the hotel. On descent, while the cabin was dimmed and the passengers snoring, he passed me a note scribbled on an airsick bag: "We've got 36 hours. Let's waste none." We didn't.

The camaraderie between gay flight attendants was its own secret society.

We knew how to spot each other in uniform—a subtle wrist flick, a too-perfect hair swoop, or the code phrase: "Are you family?"

If you knew, you knew. Sometimes we were wingmen.

Sometimes we were rivals.

Sometimes we ended up in the same bed, laughing at how small the world was. But not every story was sexy.

There were quiet moments of deep connection too. Like Jerome, a gentle soul from Atlanta who had just broken up with his long-term boyfriend. Intimately, we laid on the plush hotel carpet in Amsterdam (the texture felt like silk under our bodies), and drank sweet red wine from paper cups.

Unfortunately, our fingers barely touched because he cried about his lost dreams, and I'd rather drink a V8 with a shot of vodka. "I thought I'd be married by now," he confessed.

I didn't tell him that I once thought that, too. Hotel lobbies were undercover confessional booths. Rooftop bars became catwalks for attention and thrill seekers. Minibars were my therapists.

Inevitably, we shared our dark secrets with each other, and I doubted that anyone would have understood that our unique closets have skeletons that leased them for another three years.

Distastefully, I hated some of those moments. It was absolute hell crying alone in my hotel room on Christmas Eve. Yes, it was gut-wrenching to have a screaming match with a boyfriend via FaceTime. It was torture trying to convince myself that I was fine afterwards. No. I wasn't. In fact, I was lonely. Hell, I was alone. I was surrounded by thousands of people in a bustling city, yet I remained a ghost.

And then...there was him! My apologies, there he was! Clear out of the deep blue skies like a burst of sunshine warming your face after a lifetime of bullshit!

I won't say his name. Let's just call him "D."

D was a captain, Captain D, actually. Pun and no pun intended. He was very much older than me.

He was married and fathered three beautiful daughters. It was some real Hallmark shit, if you asked me. Personally, I liked a little spice in my life.

Inside the cockpit, just under one of the radar gadget thingamajigs, was a photo of his kids.

However, at the Marriott in Frankfurt, he kept a bottle of gin that he discreetly took to the lips to mask his untold shame and a song on his playlist called "Night Flight" was in constant rotation.

I didn't know if I liked the song or not, I was just tired of hearing it.

Initially, we started with a few drinks. Potential ass over a few shots would lure any airman to the cockpit.

Then his eager hands on my thighs sparked a reaction from my nipples because I trembled like a leaf at the start of autumn.

Afterwards, there was silence. The

dangerous kind.

Yes, the kind that made me want to pull my hair out from the roots. Yes, I should have walked away, but flight attendants were trained to handle passengers, decorum and emergencies, not our personal emotions. Not to mention he was such a skilled lover. Three times we met up in cities where no one asked questions. When our rendezvous ended, I pretended that it didn't hurt me. I tried to convince myself that I could walk away with my heart in my grasp, but for weeks, every time I boarded a plane, I half-hoped to hear him say, "This is your captain speaking..."

God, his rich baritone was like melted butter over a set of good pancakes with extra syrup drying on his mustache.

Some people I knew thought that airline drama was in the air. Nope.

The real drama happened on the ground behind hotel room doors amidst pleasurable orgasms and secret heartbreaks.

The Air and the Heartless. It was a real life soap opera, and I was the star of the show.

Even if it eventually broke my heart.

We took off. We landed But sometimes we crashed without a parachute. Then came the diplomatic charters. The ones where we assisted the White House press corps news team on the aircraft. The ones with dignitaries, senators, and the occasional "we'll tell you later" guests on the manifest was fascinating.

On one memorable flight, I served a glass of Bordeaux to a famous First Lady while I ignored the fact that her assistant kept touching my waist every time he passed through the galley. The tension was high. The flirting was higher.

Another time, I watched a journalist hook up with her cameraman in the lavatory mid-flight to Cairo, then she gave a live report an hour later with perfect hair and lipstick.

I thought, *we really are all performing.*

49

Diamonds, Diplomats & Double Lives

"Some flights weren't just about peanuts and champagne. They were about discretion. Secrets. Silent codes. And sometimes... smuggling a pouch worth more than the plane itself."

IT STARTED INNOCENTLY ENOUGH, BUT I WOULD always remember it forever. A senior flight attendant pulled me aside in the crew lounge and said, "You have the look. The calmness. The silence. Have you ever thought about doing some special runs?"

I was a bit bemused. "What is a special run?" I asked.

She gave a crooked grin. "Courier work," she said with a wink. "Off the manifest. Very hush. Very lucrative."

I smiled. "I'm listening." Months later I found myself carrying a velvet pouch sewn into the lining of my travel blazer. I chatted with a passenger while two million dollars' worth of raw diamonds rested over my heart. I never asked who sent them or where they were going. I didn't ask questions. My instructions were always precise. *Don't check the bag. Don't deviate. Don't speak about it to anyone. Smile.* And I was good at smiling. As quiet as it was kept,

I didn't transport just precious gems. There were other...transfers, classified documents and cultural artifacts. Once, I hauled a priceless watch once owned by a deposed dictator. I carried it in a Ziplock tucked beneath three pairs of Calvin Klein briefs.

Every time, my heart pounded as I passed through security checkpoints, hoping to get through without incident. My uniform was my armor. No one suspected the smiling steward with a perfectly tied tie to be smuggling anything. Unfortunately, it wasn't all glam and games. There were nights I couldn't sleep, thinking: What did I just carry? Who was I really working for? And what happened if someone decided that I knew too much?

I didn't care. Still, I never stopped. There was something intoxicating about walking through customs with a diplomatic pouch in my hand, knowing the agents wouldn't dare touch it.

I was thrilled about being trusted with silence.

And with the extra perks (luxury hotel suites, envelopes of untraceable cash, or a passionate night with a mysterious stranger named Luca who "worked in finance,") I simply minded my business. I enjoyed keeping secrets, and then I forced myself to forget them, but who cares. I was making $1,200 to $1,500 per trip. I had the sky, the secrets, and the diamonds.

50

The Flight Leader

"There's a moment during sudden turbulence where silence falls over the cabin, and you can feel every soul on that plane holding their breath. That's when you find out who you really are."

IT WAS A ROUTINE FLIGHT FROM NEW YORK to São Paulo. At least, it was supposed to be. The crew was tight and seasoned. We joked over coffee during many briefings. I was the Flight Leader on this flight, in charge of the cabin crew. The first officer was a fresh-faced kid who looked twelve in his epaulets. The captain was a legend. I loved his aviator sunglasses and slick hair. H was the kind of man who'd flown through war zones and lived to tell the tale.

We took off into a crisp blue sky, climbing smoothly above the Atlantic Ocean. After a few moments, dinner was served. The lights dimmed. Passengers curled into sleep. And then, just past midnight, 37,000 feet above the equator, The plane dropped.

Not a bump. Not a jolt. A drop. Like the Earth had been yanked out from under us.

Oxygen masks were deployed. Screams tore through the

dark cabin that made my skin crawl. A drink cart flipped over, hurling cans like missiles.

Someone shouted, "We're going down!"

I didn't even flinch. My airline flight attendant training took over. I grabbed the intercom, and barked into it. "Keep your seatbelts fastened and Flight Attendants please secure the cabin and remain in your jump seats."

Then I checked the aisles. People were praying, weeping, and clinging to complete strangers.

Calmly, I knelt beside a hyperventilating man and whispered, "Breathe with me. I'm not leaving you."

I wasn't acting, I was performing. In that moment, I was the show. And if I remained calm, they believed they were safe.

The aircraft shook like a paper kite. Lightning lit the cabin with violent flashes.

Over the PA, the captain's voice cut in, steady but grim:

"Ladies and gentlemen, please remain seated. We are experiencing severe turbulence. We have control of the aircraft." He didn't lie, but he didn't tell the whole truth either.

Later, I found out that one of the engines had temporarily lost thrust.

We were flying blind through a thunderstorm.

Plus, air traffic control had lost contact with us for six terrifying minutes.

Six minutes. That's all it took to confront everything I'd been avoiding. In those six minutes, I thought of my grandmother. I pictured her rosary in her hand as she waved me off for my first flight. I thought of the men and women I'd loved and lost.

I thought of the Dubai skyline I never got to paint, the child I never adopted, and the letter I never sent to my birth mother.

Then, I thought of my crew. So, I unbuckled my safety belt, went against protocol, and staggered through the cabin to help a junior FA who was frozen in fear near the lavatories.

I gripped her shoulders. "You were born for this. This is what we were trained for. Do your job. We're going to make it."

She nodded, and just like that—she was back.

When landed hard, fast, and safe in São Paulo, the entire plane burst into applause. I didn't smile. I just exhaled.

Later, in the hotel room, I stripped off my uniform and stood under the hottest shower I could stand. I didn't cry. I just let the water wash away the sweat, the fear, the what-ifs.

The next morning, someone slid a handwritten note under my door. It was the passenger from seat 3A, a middle-aged woman who'd sobbed into my shoulder mid-flight. She was staying at our layover hotel.

It read: "Thank you. Your voice was the only thing keeping me sane. You saved me."

I was a waiter in the sky, a lifeguard in the clouds, a crisis manager in heels and the last calm face people might ever see.

And that night, I met the strongest version of myself.
Not the one who wore designer scarves or flirted in first class, but the one who stood tall when the sky fell.

51
Scandal at 30,000 feet

"I knew the truth. The press knew the rumors. But only the clouds knew what really happened behind that curtain."

PAN AM HAD A CONTRACT WITH THE NBA. We took basketball players to and from their games. The fellows got to know you, and you, them. They were treated like celebrities, and we served them. There were the seasoned players and the rookies who were young and just recruited. It just so happened that one of the players, a rookie, took a liking to me.

He always came in the back to the galley to ask for something. Since he was new, I told him there was a flight attendant call button above his seat and all he had to do was press the button and a flight attendant would assist him.

I was extremely professional, and the Pan Am charter department had strict rules about our conduct while dealing with the players. We could not ask for autographs, or take photos and a few NDA items we had to sign.

The lavatories were located at the rear of the aircraft and right by the galley. Sometimes the seasoned guy would peek their heads in and say hello.

We normally closed a curtain which separated the galley from the passengers. It was usually done after we finished the meal and beverage service. This was to give them privacy.

There were coaches strategizing playbooks and most of the players had Walkmans (this was the 1980s) and their devices where they play video games and whatever else they do.

About a month into the season, we all started getting personal. John, the rookie who I told about the call button, came back to the galley, perfectly timed while the other flight attendants were busy. He said that I had hurt his feelings when I told him to ring his call button. I apologized and told him that new rookies didn't know about the button, and we didn't want players being inconvenienced by having to get up to ask for a drink or something else when it was our job to do.

He said okay and that sometimes he wanted to say hello but to him it looked like I was purposely not looking in his direction.

I then asked if he needed something and he said "Yes, I

want to talk to you because I think you are an interesting person and very mysterious."

I couldn't help but laugh and he started laughing too. I asked him what he would like to know, and he said that he would rather talk to me off-the-record. So, he gave me his phone number, and I did the same thing.

I had an idea about what this was, but decided to play the game. And I was right. He started to get personal, and he asked if I had a girlfriend. I said, "No, I don't but do you have one?"

And he said, "No."

Anyway, we decided to meet at a small cafe hidden in Chinatown, New York. We talked about everything and then we started to get serious. We started dating and it lasted 8 years without anyone knowing... or so we thought.

The rumors started from a whisper. One of the flight attendants on our crew showed me a tabloid headline during passenger boarding at JFK airport. It was Page 6 news, the gossip columnist's famous page. It read: "NBA Star's Secret Jet Romance—Who's the Mystery Man?"

The grainy photo showed the silhouette of two men in an airport lounge. One was unmistakably John. The other was a cropped figure with broad shoulders, tailored slacks, and a watch I had gotten in Rome. A Patek Phillipe. I nearly dropped the coffee pot. I had always known our relationship was on limited time.

He was the crown jewel of a major basketball franchise. I was just the man behind the beverage cart. Our world had no space for honesty. We were lustful shadows enshrouded in secrecy, and luxury penthouse suites with the curtains drawn were our musical playgrounds.

For eight years, we played the game. Red-eye flights to meet in Miami were to die for. Alias names on hotel bookings was our reality. Wrist brushes in limousines turned me on. There were messages that disappeared after reading them.

But someone had seen us. Someone had spilled the beans.

And now, the tabloids were circling us like vultures with microphones. Eventually, the airline had called me into the office.

Corporate Affairs. It was a closed-door meeting. Unfortunately, no coffee and tea was offered. "Is

it true?" I was asked by the director. I

didn't blink. "Is what true?"

He didn't smile. "Don't play coy with me. You were

assigned to John's private charters. There are photos. We need a statement."

I laughed, a little too hard. "You want a statement? Fine: I served him hot towels, and he liked two sugars in his tea. Is that scandalous enough for you?"

He didn't seem convinced, but I wasn't a snitch.

Meanwhile, the headlines became glaringly louder.

Flight Risk: NBA Star's High-Flying Affair Could Threaten Career.
Mystery Man Identified?
Sources Say He Was "Part of the Flight Crew"

They never printed my name, but it was out there. And the fallout was inevitable. Giving me the side eye, my colleagues avoided me in the lounge.

Those I thought were cordial became gossipmongers. A few associates snickered behind my back like small-minded peasants. I kept to myself and became somewhat of an introvert with my personal business. I refused to feed into the noise.

Thankfully, there were some kind people in the bunch of spoiled apples. They quietly slipped me notes that said, "I get it.

Stay strong," to paraphrase, but the damage was done.

I was now a scandal in uniform. Private whispers within my space didn't get a reaction out of me. It was a cautionary tale I never entertained or fed into. I kept a poker face, and yes, I was still a sight to see.

After some time, I reached out to my secret NBA lover only once after our affair became mainstream. My hands trembled as I dialed his number. I wanted to hang up before it rang, but I couldn't bring myself to do it. I needed to hear his voice, knowing that his baritone would immediately set me on fire.

He answered on the first ring. "I'm

sorry," he said rather blandly.

Say that you love me! Say that you'll come out of the closet and give me everything you promised me in private just before you had to cum!

"I know," I replied, swallowing the lump in my throat. "I

didn't want this," he whispered.

The tears fell from my eyes and soaked into the fabric of my blazer. "Neither did I," I lied.

Unfortunately, we never spoke again. Eight years, gone like a puff of smoke from a crackpipe. Broken, shaken and betrayed, I stood in front of the aircraft mirror before my first flight away from a life I'd never know again. There was a moment when I almost called him back, but my body became a block of ice, and I just couldn't. I didn't chase anyone, they chased me.

I fixed my tie, straightened my uniform and stepped back onto that plane like nothing had ever happened. Deep inside I was enraged! I wanted to break things, punch someone, scream out loud but I was a gentleman. I wasn't trained to perform through the turbulence that came with mixing business with pleasure.

Even when the turbulence was my broken heart wrapped in my ex-lover's Versace cologne. Maybe the passengers thought I was just another smiling face handing out pretzels just doing his job, but I was a wreck.

They didn't see the scandal, the shame, or the shards of the life I'd tried so hard to keep private because he asked me to.

And pounded me into a thousand orgasms, each more intense than the last.

I was whipped, and completely under his spell.

Especially his bedroom eyes. Just one look into mine I felt the tingles in my thighs while he was deep inside me, controlling my spine.

My co-workers and the passengers of flight 234 saw my charm. I was still poised. I was still in control of my integrity.

And that was exactly what I gave them. What they paid for.

Excellent customer service.

When you were a dedicated flight attendant, remember the golden rule.

No matter how hard I fell in love, I always kept my landing gear. And a parachute, when it was mission, abort.

52

Fired, Famous and flawlessly vindicated

THE CELEBRITY SCANDAL INVOLVING MY secret romance in the newspapers were written and published by vultures that sensationalized fragments of my broken heart. Watching it all unfold nearly tore me apart. For eight years my ex-lover and I experienced what I thought was love, but only behind the scenes. We were so damn careful, yet the alleged truth came out anyway.

Was it really about lust with me and him? In private we live out loud, but I was tamed by the reality that we could never be together because of his lucrative career. It blew my mind how big the story had grown.

They were not letting it go. In fact, it had gotten worse when it reached the corporate offices of Pan Am, jeopardizing my livelihood. It had my undivided attention.

My superiors didn't fire me, but I was grounded (put out of work) for a week, pending an investigation. Just my damn luck. I didn't give an explanation, nor did I offer recourse. I let it all play out because chess was more enthralling than dominoes and checkers.

The headlines about the NBA player, my ex-lover, gave Pan Am Airlines unsolicited heat in their Corporate Communications department. After the investigation, a meeting was called with my union leader. My superiors had made their decision.

"Immediate termination due to a Breach in my Code of Conduct."

What? I had to hand in my company ID card, my CID credentials, my cockpit door key and my wings while they masked slight grins. I was deeply upset. How could everything I worked so hard for go up in flames?

What would my friends, associates and colleagues think? I knew that my grandmother was turning in her grave and there was no way I was letting them fuck me over and didn't get treated to breakfast in bed, like I'd done for my ex-lover, the famous ballplaying asshole that left me alone in the charade to clean up the mess. I was a flight attendant, not a maid. I didn't clean up shit, I flushed it.

In spite of everything, I still polished my crown even though I cried myself to sleep over a near decade of romance changing in an instant.

There wasn't a goodbye party thrown in my honor nor was

I looking for one. My pension, kaboom! Gone, like my sex life I'd become addicted to. Now I was going through withdrawal and relationship hell.

He was an excellent glass of Scotch after a grueling day in the real world, only his milkshake all over my body was the best massage lotion I ever used. It was why my skin sun kissed the sky when I ventured throughout my day.

I was given a stiff termination letter citing "conduct unbecoming" and "violations of company policy."

I thought it was unfair. They couldn't prove that I breached the contract I signed to become a flight attendant. My name had never appeared in the press, but gossiping scallywags 'were desperate to wash their hands of the scandal.

Unfortunately for my superiors, I didn't go quietly. I sued them. Hard. My claim? Wrongful termination. No documentation. It turned out that they never investigated anything.

They believed the hearsay. They displayed homophobia dressed up as policy enforcement. I found a fierce attorney, a gay Cuban firebrand with a flair for media attention. We filed a federal lawsuit. The story caught fire.

Within a couple of weeks, I was the headline.

"Flight Attendant Sues Airline Over Secret Firing Tied to NBA Affair" "David vs Goliath at 35,000 Feet."

I became a cause. An icon. The face of the unfairly grounded. To my dismay, the case dragged on for months. The airline scrambled. They didn't have any emails. No photos. No policy violations. Only the discomfort with who I was and who I had been loving.

Passengers were writing letters about my character; frequent flier Medallion members voiced their opinion for me to be re-instated.

Pan Am couldn't control the overwhelming public responses from civil rights leaders, the NAACP, GLAD, HRC. The negative publicity was causing a disruption to its reputation.

Their lawyers blinked first, then dissolved like wet tissue. We settled rather quickly. I knew it was only to protect their brand and maintain their superficial image. The terms? I would be reinstatement, though I had no intention of staying long. I get full back pay with interest and a very generous settlement figure, sealed under an NDA. It was $50K, which in the 80's was good money. And just like that—I was back. But I wasn't finished with them.

"Hell hath no fury like a male flight attendant scorned"

53
Payback Is A Bitch!

THERE WAS A TICKET AGENT AT JFK I'D ALWAYS been friendly with.
Let's call him "Nick." He was extremely handsome, married with
kids, but always flirted with me a little too long for a straight man. He
flew often, and whenever he did, I'd upgrade him to
First Class without blinking. Well, now it was my turn. One night
over drinks, I told him I had a wild idea.

"Write me a ticket," I said. "Something deluxe. Concorde-
level. Something I'll tell my grandkids about."

He laughed. But I didn't. "Just this once," I whispered.
"You know I'd do it for you."

And so, he did. He was now in a supervisory role and knew
what to do. The next week, I was seated aboard the British Airways
Concorde from JFK-London's Heathrow airport.

I brought Simone with me, of course. She'd always had my
back, and I needed someone who could keep a secret.

We arrived in London from New York in under four hours.

We shared Dom Perignon champagne in Baccarat crystal
flutes and ate from Wedgewood plates.

Velvet seats.

A few affluent passengers asked was I oil-tycoon royalty.

We saw Elizabeth Taylor and Joan Collins, so I went up to them and told them how much I loved their work. Of course, they asked what I did for a living.

I told them I was an airline executive for Pan Am.

From London, we had open First Class tickets. They were handwritten, just like in the old days, with no digital trail. I filled them in myself, but that was not the only tickets that were written.

We had four open positive space "must ride" diplomatic tickets as well.

Those tickets were only used by the Chairman, CEO, Board Members and other elites. If there was a full paying passenger who had actually paid for their tickets for first class, then they would be downgraded to Club Class to accommodate us in first class with "those" tickets.

No questions asked.

The flight crew was from London, so nobody knew who we were, the New Yorkers.

We were treated like royalty, and that definitely took the edge off of my pain.

The Pursers and flight attendants all knew that VIP Elites

were on board based on our "P1" code. My

itinerary was breathtaking:

London to Nairobi.

I fed giraffes at dawn and watched the sun set over the savannah.

Nairobi to Cape Town.

I stood at the gates of Robben Island, and ran my hands over the bars that once

caged Mandela.

Cape Town to Sydney.

I sipped wine overlooking the Harbour Bridge, danced with strangers, visited the

Opera House and saw "Aida" and woke up barefoot on Bondi Beach.

Sydney to New York.

Back to reality, richer in experience and scandalously unbothered by the bullshit of the

past.

Simone and I made a toast after every takeoff. We laughed until our cheeks ached. We flew back on the Air France Concorde. With my perfect French I was able to convince the agent to change our tickets.

We lived like we had nothing to lose because Pan Am would never find out.

And then, sure enough within nine months... they were gone. Pan Am filed for bankruptcy. I did a backflip and a full split knowing damn well if I attempted such theatrics I'd pull my back out. I'd rather lay under a good joystick and get it blown out.

The airline ceased operations. *Hallelujah!* The archives burned in a blaze of debt and mismanagement. Me and Simone's $20,000 global joyride vanished with it.

It was undocumented, untraceable, and untouchable.

Ah!

Revenge was best served cold with a shot of brandy.

My silent vengeance manifested into the form of leather seats, smoked salmon, hors d'oeuvres, and a private moment watching the stars from 38,000 feet... knowing that I beat the system with style.

And I didn't even have to offer a statement....

Or feed into the celebrity gossip that eventually faded into other scandalous celebrities doing things that made me blush.

I just moved differently. I wasn't like most guys.

Especially if you pissed me off.

54

The Day the World's Greatest Airline Fell

PAN AM AIRLINES WAS MORE THAN A JOB. IT WAS MY identity, a crown, and a calling in my life. I looked forward to going to work every time the sun rose. I wore my navy blues with pride, walked through international terminals like royalty, and knew our place in the world was thirty thousand feet above it.

Then, in 1991, the unthinkable happened. Pan American World Airways went bankrupt. I knew it was going to happen.

Sixty-thousand of us were suddenly grounded. Our salaries were persona non grata: gone. Thousands of pensions vaporized, benefits erased like we'd never existed.

I remembered staring at the television as the news broke, my body numb. We had given our youth, our holidays, and our hearts to this company.

We were the elite. The world used to bow to the Pan Am logo.

Now, we were just unemployed.

197 | Kurt Hanson

The heartbreak was universal, but my survival was personal. Everyone scrambled. Some people took temp jobs; others tried to pivot different careers.

A few fell into depression, unable to imagine a life without boarding passes and jet engines. We became a displaced tribe of once-gilded wanderers, cast out of the sky.

But not Pat W.

Pat W was a legend in her own right. She was a flight attendant manager with the poise of a queen and the resolve of a general.

I had a lot of love and adoration for her. In my opinion she had a heart of gold and went after what she wanted in life and didn't make excuses for it.

She had an eye for talent, a sharp tongue, and a soft spot for the best of the best because she was the best.

She was fluent in multiple languages, with a Rolodex that could put the CIA to shame.

Pat W wasn't going down on the ship.

Within months, she secured a leadership position at TWA Airlines, and like a phoenix, she rose—and brought twenty-five of us with her.

We were her chosen few.

We were the multilingual, high-standard, first-class trained attendants who knew how to navigate diplomacy at 37,000 feet.

I was honored and grateful to be on her list. Suddenly, we had uniforms again.

Boarding passes. Flight benefits.

We were back in the sky—but everything had changed. TWA was no Pan Am.

The aircraft felt older, and the routes were less glamorous. The culture was more chaotic, but we made it work. We brought Pan Am polish to every cabin.

We turned coach into couture.

We were surviving and elevating together.

For three years, we gave TWA our all.

And then it happened again.

TWA filed for bankruptcy.

It was déjà vu, karma, and devastation with a side of betrayal. The carpet ripped from under us, again.

Only this time, we were a little bitter, a little more hardened, and a lot less naïve.

But once again, Pat W moved swiftly. She
had secured another lifeline.

Northwest Airlines, based in Minneapolis.

And once again, she took her favorites.

55

Pat W's Chosen Few

Northwest Airlines
Class # 10, 1999
FRONT ROW: L to R: Gary Powell - Instructor, Mollie Carlson - Instructor, Ryan Brothers - Instructor. ROW 2: Katie Quinlan, Karine Wedel, Kurt Hansen, Patricia Rice - Manager, William Nour, Alice Evans, Karen McEnany.

NORTHWEST AIRLINES DIDN'T HAVE THE sparkle of Pan Am, or even the legacy of TWA, but it had structure and stability. For Pat W, it had potential, and that meant potential opportunities for us. She was the definition of reaching back and helping someone else up. She was selfless by default. She fought hard to bring us on board. "My chosen few have a multilingual advantage," she informed the higher ups, "international finesse, *and* gold-standard training."

"Why should we trust your chosen few?"

"Because it will be a great disservice to recruit some of the best flight attendants in the world."

She had their attention then. Thankfully, Northwest reluctantly agreed.

Unfortunately, there was a catch. We had to go through eight long ass weeks of full flight attendant training and learn everything we already knew.

We would be starting from scratch with twenty-somethings who had never seen the inside of a 747, let alone served caviar and vodka at 38,000 feet in the air. We were seasoned professionals, being asked to earn our wings again. Drama was brooding on the horizon, and I felt the icy chill, a prelude of things to come.

We were flown to Northwest's training academy that was located outside Minneapolis. It was a sprawling, gray-toned facility with all the security of a government building. The air was cold, and the mood was icy. We weren't properly greeted. You'd swear we were refugees seeking asylum in their country. The instructors made it very clear to us (with an attitude) this was not Pan Am.

Where was the lie? *That*, we agreed on. They couldn't hold a candle to the legacy of Pan Am.

From the moment we stepped off the shuttle, I felt the tension. We were outsiders. They were envious that we were older, and more refined. Some of us had accents and attitudes the trainers weren't ready for.

The younger trainees talked about us like a dog, but never to our faces. The staff always eyed us with suspicion. They saw Pat

W's group as a clique of divas. And what if we were? Who was going to check us, Boo? They had no idea what they were in for.

We were about to enter a battleground of egos, expectations, and endurance. This was training and a test of will. And not all of us would make it through.

The drama begins in the next chapter.

56

The Class That Almost Wasn't

THERE I WAS AGAIN! BACK IN FLIGHT ATTENDANT training. Ugh! This time around it wasn't the glamor of Pan Am or the prestige of TWA. This was Northwest Airlines, an airline with a sprawling fleet, a serious tone, and a reputation for chewing up and spitting out the most seasoned crew members.

Eight weeks. Sixteen types of aircrafts. Thirty-five trainees. That was the battlefield.

The first day was all introductions. We were a mixture of rookies, and survivors from defunct airlines (Pan-Am, Eastern, Braniff, Midway). The eldest senior was Katie, who logged twenty years with Eastern airlines before they folded.

The age range ran from fresh-faced twenty-somethings to silver-haired veterans pushing sixty.

Northwest had inherited planes like they were heirlooms. There were DC-9s, MD-80s, L-1011s, 727s, 757s, 747s, and Airbus A300s. We had to know everything. And I did mean everything.

We were housed in a Northwest-owned training complex

in Eden Prairie, Minneapolis, surrounded by manicured lawns, a nearby mall, and most importantly, a liquor store.

My roommate was Jermaine, a charismatic party animal who had flown for Ryanair airlines. He brought the fire, the chaos, and the charm. The rules were annoying. We were observed inside and outside of the classroom. Every module ended in an exam. Anything under 85% was an epic fail. Three fails and you were terminated.

And the housing rules? We couldn't have guests. No pool parties past 10 p.m. Weekends? Meant for studying. The pool may have looked inviting, but behind that serenity lurked a trap.

By Week 3, the pressure mounted. We had already lost a few classmates because they failed their tests. That Saturday, Jermaine and a group organized a get-together to relieve the pressure of those tests.

There were drinks, music, and laughter. It was innocent enough, until they decided to take the party to the pool after hours.

Once security closed and chained the area, they scaled the fence and kept the party going. I had a bad feeling and bowed out early, sensing trouble. Thank God.

Because Monday morning, the storm hit. We arrived to class early and we were called, one by one, to the training manager's office.

The rest of us had to wait in the cafeteria. The unease was suffocating.

When we finally returned to the classroom, twelve desks were empty.

Just like that, they were gone.

Terminated.

It sent a shockwave through the rest of us.

The energy shifted. In the weeks that followed, the tests were harder.

We lost three more people. One by one, they failed. I was heartbroken because in my mind all of us was going to succeed, but that wasn't the case.

By the start of Week 8, there were nine of us left. By graduation day? Six.

We had made history because of the graduating class size. Class 4 of 1999, the smallest graduating class in Northwest Airlines' history.

By 2001, I was the only one left. A few of my acquaintances quit, and the others didn't pass the probationary period.

Jermaine eventually got hired by American Airlines. Katie? I saw her years later on one of my flights. She was visiting her granddaughter in Philadelphia.

Time had moved on, but that bond from Eden Prairie lingered.

Those eight weeks bonded us together like family. I left with a sense of pride.

Because my career wasn't handed to me. I

earned it.

57
The Sister in the Lounge

SIX MONTHS AFTER TRAINING, I HAD TRANSFERRED from Minneapolis
to Detroit, settling into my new base. The snow, the bustle, the
crews....everything had the scent of fresh beginnings. I was finding my
rhythm again.

One afternoon, I checked in late for a flight, a serious
offense in the airline world. I headed to my supervisor's office to
explain myself.

Imagine my surprise when I ran into Pat W, my old
manager from Pan Am and TWA.

She was also my supervisor at Northwest. She was in the
middle of a meeting, with another flight attendant waiting ahead of
me in line.

Pat W was handling another flight attendant while a third
woman waited in line ahead of me. We exchanged the usual polite
hellos. She looked familiar, but I couldn't place her. Her name tag
read Mrs. C. Handke, a German surname.

Nothing rang a bell. When Pat W emerged and asked who

was next, I motioned to the woman beside me.

"She was here before me."

Pat W smiled and said casually, "Have you met Kirt? He was one of my chosen few from Pan Am and TWA."

She turned and looked at me, really looked. Puzzled, she narrowed her eyes and looked me over with a curiosity I couldn't understand.

There was a strange familiarity in her gaze. Like someone walking through a dream they couldn't quite manage.

Claudette Handke.

The name didn't mean anything to me. But that face... there was something.

Now, Claudette was a bit of a legend at Northwest airlines.

Everyone knew about the high-society Purser who lived in Frankfurt and commuted eight hours to Detroit like it was a short drive to the mall.

I had heard her name for years, but I had no idea who she really was. Until the snowstorm. Detroit came to a grinding halt. No flights in, no flights out.

The crew lounge was packed with stranded flight attendants grumbling about delays, missing connections, and cold vending machine coffee.

I was waiting for my flight to Fort Lauderdale. Claudette was trying to get home to Germany.

She was within earshot as I chatted with my crew mates. Something I said must've triggered something because she walked over and began asking questions.

Innocent ones at first. Where
did I live?

Where did I go to school? The
usual idle snow-day talk.

Then she said something that cracked the shell:

"I'm from Jamaica... with my grandmother. On an estate called Moreton Park."

I blinked.

"I own Moreton Park," I said quietly. She
stared at me. Silence fell between us.

I added slowly, "I had a sister named Claudette Williamson. She left Jamaica when I was ten to study psychology in New Jersey."

She took a few steps back, visibly shaken. "That's
my maiden name," she said.

I frowned, still unsure. "But you have a German name now. Claudette would be... Claudette James."

"I married Davin James. We divorced ten years ago." My mouth fell open.

The room spun.

Could this really be Claudette? Still, doubt clung to me like static. There had to be proof.

Something only the two of us would know.

So, I went for it. "My Claudette bought me a dog..."

Before I could finish the sentence, she gasped and said, "A black and brown dachshund. Her name was Sheeba."

And that was it. The floodgates broke.

I didn't even feel myself walking toward her with my arms stretched. The next thing I knew, I was crying and hugging her, my voice shaking.

My heart hammered in disbelief.

The lounge had gone completely still.

Dozens of stunned flight attendants stared, some with tears in their eyes, others blinking in shock.

Claudette turned to the crowd and announced, "I just found my brother... after twenty-seven years."

The rest was a whirlwind. We went straight to Pat W's office. She sat in silence, taking it in. Then she smiled softly and said, "I'm not surprised. You both carry yourselves the same way. That same sophistication."

Somehow, corporate communications caught wind of it (we suspected it might have been Pat W.) A week later, there was a note in both our mailboxes. They wanted to feature our story in the airline's onboard magazine *and* the company newsletter.

Soon, passengers were reading about us, sipping tomato juice and marveling at our reunion like it was a fairytale in the sky.

Employees began stopping us in terminals, gate areas, even mid-flight. *"Are you the siblings from the magazine?"*

"Tell us the story!"

At first it was touching.

Then it became overwhelming. The attention, the whispers, the constant retelling, it became our dark cloud.

We started flying together, sometimes to Paris.

I'd serve as the French interpreter; she was still the regal Purser. And without fail, someone on the crew would smile knowingly.

"I just flew with your sister."

"Your brother's on my flight next week."

Eventually, the frenzy died down.

But the bond never did.

After nearly three decades of silence and distance, fate (helped along by snow, a name tag, and Sheeba the dog) stitched us back together in a flight attendant lounge on a day no planes could fly because of the snowstorm.

58

The Beginning of Northwest Airline World Travels

"I had lovers in languages I didn't speak, cried under domes older than Jesus, and kissed strangers who smelled like sandalwood and secrets."

AS FLIGHT ATTENDANTS, PEOPLE TREATED YOU with respect, like royalty. Dressed in our uniforms, heads held high, people were impressed with the notion that we had a job that was glamorous and knew that we were world travelers.

On flights, there were secret exchanges of phone numbers from both men and women, written on napkins or their business cards. There would be whispers of meetings at our layover hotels, invitations to dinner, the movies, or the hope of spending the night with them.

On one trip to Cairo, I met Mohammed. He was very pleasant. He asked how long my layover was. When I told him forty-eight hours, he asked if he could be my tour guide.

We had landed in Cairo, and I had barely slept. Not

because of the time zone, but because Omar, the charming Egyptian doctor I'd been chatting with for two weeks on a dating site, had shown up at my hotel like a scene out of Casablanca.

He brought Turkish delight and bold wine. I brought my sexiness and curiosity. But I had to juggle him and Mohammed together.

That was the thing about being a flight attendant. Loneliness was our permanent carry-on. We packed it with our street clothes, and when we landed in foreign cities, we unpacked it with a glass of something strong and someone who smelled unfamiliar.

Hook-up websites were our little secret. It was discreet, digital and a lifeline. You talked to them for days before a layover, let that flirtation grow, and then, like clockwork, you met in the lobby bar or the back entrance of the hotel. Intimacy was a thrill, so was anonymity.

Omar was different though. His voice had depth, and when he whispered "Enti helwa," I believed him, even if I wasn't sure what it meant.

That morning, he took me to the pyramids before sunrise. The city hadn't yet woken. The air was still, and the desert stretched out like something biblical.

The Sphinx was smaller than I imagined, but more majestic. As we stood together under the awakening sun, I felt something crack open in me. The kind of silence that only came after you'd had too much life, too much lust, too much distance between flights.

He kissed my temple. I almost cried.

From Cairo, I flew to Delhi. The place was a loud, layered chaos of color and incense. The smell of marigolds clung to everything, even our uniforms. My crew and I stayed in a heritage hotel that once housed British diplomats and, according to the concierge, several friendly ghosts.

India wasn't a layover. It was an awakening. At the Taj Mahal, I wore a red sherwani I'd bought from a market stall. I wanted to blend in, but the truth was, no one ever really blended in there. The mausoleum shimmered like it was lit from the inside. I touched the cold marble, and thought about the emperor who built it for love, and the men who died building it.

I thought about Omar. And I thought about another man, a poet from Mumbai I'd had a coffee date with just the day before. He read Neruda and told me my eyes looked like "trouble on a slow simmer."

We'd kissed behind a mango cart. That was the rhythm of

it all. Love. History. Goodbye.

In Istanbul, the smell of cardamom and fresh bread nearly knocked me over. We wandered through the Grand Bazaar like wild women, flight attendants unleashed.

We bartered for scarves and silver, and I ended up with a man named Halil who sold rugs and had a smile too white to be legal. He took me to a rooftop overlooking the Bosphorus. We drank arak until our teeth were numb. He told me stories about the Ottoman Empire while I sat in his lap, watching the mosques light up one by one. The call to prayer echoed across the city like a lullaby. I didn't love him. I didn't need to. But he gave me memories and tenderness that night that I carried until this day.

Being a flight attendant, I never stayed in one place too long, but I lived more in a 24-hour layover than most people did in years. I saw sunsets from the steps of Petra, had my palm read in the alley behind a Moroccan spice shop, and danced barefoot on the stones of Jerusalem until my knees gave out.

In every city, I found a version of myself I didn't know existed. No matter how many takeoffs or landings, parts of me would remain scattered across the sand, the silk, the spice markets, and the men who whispered promises I never expected to keep.

Ever.

59
Visual Reflections (Photos)

Kurt Hanson and Cynthia Bailey (RHOA)

Kurt, Andy and Rosie at the GLAAD Awards

Kurt Hanson & Claudette (reunited with his sister)

*Kurt Hanson and Basketball
Superstar Shaquille O'Neal*

Kurt Hanson and Tara

Kurt Hanson and a Dubai Royal Prince

"*Karma's A Basketball Bitch*" book

Kurt Hanson. Opera singer. Jamaica. 1979

60
Cruising Altitude & Cold Wars

ASSISTING PASSENGERS ON THE MOST ELITE routes came with its perks. There were five-star layovers, celebrity passengers, and hotel suites with bathtubs bigger than most apartments. But behind the caviar service and crisp linen napkins, there was another class war brewing. Not in first class, but in the galley.

The Senior Mamas. Yes, those old motherfuckers who sat in the galley gossiping and not working. Those older female flight attendants with forty years under their girdles. Their beehive hair was stiff as helmets, and their scowls were etched across their faces. They ruled the aisles like bitter monarchs, clinging to their seniority numbers like thrones, and they hated us younger flight attendants because we came polished and ready to evolve.

They saw us as threats. We were too good-looking, too quick, and too polished. They rolled their eyes at our enthusiasm, mocked our smiles, and barked orders like drill sergeants on a power trip.

God forbid if you touched their coffee pot or rearranged their galley cart.

"You're not here to flirt, honey," one of them hissed at me during a red-eye to Milan. "You're here to serve."

I smiled sweetly. "I can do both. Multitasking was covered in my 4 airline trainings. That's why I am Kirt the Flirt." I said sarcastically while throwing them a dirty look as if to say, "Don't fuck with me. I'm the wrong one."

But their pettiness ran deep.

They'd dump the worst sections on us.

The economy middle rows, crying baby zones, and the drunk businessmen in coach was the worst, and then the Senior Mamas would disappear behind the curtain with a tabloid and a tray of leftover chocolates.

Meanwhile, we worked in the aisles like marathoners.

Sometimes our feet blistered, but our smiles were plastered on our faces with caffeine and pure willpower.

And if you were assigned first class? Oh, the claws came out.

Because first class wasn't just about better seats.

It was prestige. Performance. Tips. Access.

The kind of access that made headlines...or secrets.

There was the oil tycoon who requested me by name after I

offered him a hot towel and a joke.

He gave me a Cartier watch the next time we flew. "You remind me of someone special," he said. "You're my favorite."

There was a royal (actual royalty) who slipped me his private number on a cocktail napkin folded into a swan.

And then there were the athletes.

Six-foot-something towers of muscle and ego, flying on chartered jets with private chefs and brand-new entourages each week.

They wanted everything fast. Food, service, attention. And they got it. Always. Because their tips could pay off your rent for two months. Because their fame made them untouchable.

The senior ladies hated it.

They hated how easily those passengers gravitated toward us. They *hated* the way we laughed and glided down the aisle like we were born to be adored.

They hated that we made the job look fun while they trudged along like prison guards in polyester.

But here's what they never understood. We weren't just handsome, young and fresh faces, we were hustlers. Survivors. Attendants who'd fought through immigration lines, passport lines, broken hearts, and impossible odds to get those wings.

While they sat bitter in their jump-seats, thumbing through gossip magazines, I was making connections. Stashing stories. Building a world of secrets that no one could take from me.

They may have had seniority, but I was the future.

.

61

The Hidden Side of Sports Charters

I WAS TAPPED FOR SOMETHING EXCLUSIVE: sports charters. Something I had done already and almost got fired for it at Pan Am. It wasn't just a promotion; it was an induction into a world where the rich and famous played by their own rules. It wasn't immediate.

It would be 10 years after doing my international flights that I would be chosen. But that would come later on.

The committee that chose the crew didn't just look for skills, they looked for people who could keep their mouths shut. Well, who better to know the rules, than me.

I knew the routine, but luckily my Pan Am experience was a distant memory. But this what I realized...the real show didn't happen on the court or the field, it happened in the sky.

But I already knew it and this time I was prepared.

Flying with professional athletes was like being backstage at a rock concert that never ended.

On game nights, the energy was electric.

The locker room didn't stop at the stadium, it spilled onto the plane, where the celebrations were just beginning.

Expensive champagne flowed like water, cigars were lit without a second thought, and players loosened their ties (sometimes literally) letting the tension of the game melt away.

But when they lost it was a different story.

I witnessed locker room fights spill over into the cabin, players hurling fists and expletives at each other, bruises forming before we even reached cruising altitude.

Once, an enraged player punched a window so hard I thought it would crack.

Another time, I saw a coach grab a player by the collar, screaming in his face while the rest of the team watched in stunned silence.

The off-the-court action was just as wild. I saw star players kissing their side pieces on the tarmac while their wives and kids were at home, oblivious.

I helped smooth over emergencies, like the time one of the biggest names in the NBA realized he left his wedding ring in the hotel room he'd just shared with someone who wasn't his wife.

I made a call and flew to Philly on my day off to give him his ring back.

And then there was the night I found myself in the middle of a scandal that could've ended careers.

A player (married, high-profile, beloved) came to me in a panic.

His mistress had left something in his bag—a very personal item. Oh, what the hell.

It was her panty.

I had to act fast, slipping it into my own bag, pretending it was mine, and disposing of it before his wife found it.

That was the night I realized: in this world, you weren't just a flight attendant.

You were a fixer, a confidante, and sometimes, an accomplice.

Did I want to be part of their scandal and lies, of course not, but I did what I had to do to ensure that every passenger was treated with dignity and respect, no matter what they did on and off the aircraft.

I was loyal, as loyal as they came.

Maybe that was why elite passengers, politicians and moneyed passengers gravitated towards me. I was different.

I moved different. I knew how to keep my mouth shut. I knew how to turn the other check.

I knew how to mind my own business. I knew how to keep a poker face.

I knew the ends and the outs, especially after the scandal I went through with Pan Am.

I knew how to play the game.

62
Here We Go Again!

HERE I GO AGAIN. DIDN'T I LEARN MY LESSON the first time. I never should have fallen for him. He was an NBA legend, and I was just part of the crew. But when he looked at me like I was the only guy in the world, I was powerless to resist.

It all started two months after he was traded from another team. For him, having a casual conversation was nothing, but if other players suspected you were talking to a guy rather than one of the girls, then you wouldn't hear the end of it.

And I warned him, but he said he didn't care. He would leave his seat to come to the galley to ask for cranberry juice.

Yes, as I was taught, explain the flight attendant call button. I told him that he could have just pressed his flight attendant call button and one of us would have come to him, but his excuse was always that he needed to stretch his legs.

He was almost seven- feet tall so I understood.

However, I had learned from doing trips with downlow athletes that their mode of operation was very coy and well-rehearsed. It normally started off with small talk, then they wanted to know what you normally did on your days off, what hobbies did you like?

And then the all-important question, "So, what are you into?"

It was a cat and mouse game that was so worn out. Usually, my response was that I was there to do my job and made sure you were comfortable going to and from your games. But this time, it was different.

Those piercing eyes, his big hands, his rugged looks and polite mannerisms made it difficult for me.

He wasn't like the others.

He was thuggish, humble and well-mannered. Qualities you didn't typically find in other players. He was usually listening to music or playing a video game.

I gave him his cranberry juice, and he slipped me a piece of paper with his phone number.

I knew I would be seeing him often, so I really didn't think too much of it.

About three weeks later, his team was on my roster. He was

acting really strange. I greeted everyone, including him, and he ignored me.

I thought nothing of it but carried on with serving their meals and drinks. The flight was two hours long, and we had finished the service early to allow them time to rest.

They all knew to ring their flight attendant call-button. But they would end up at the galley.

I was sitting on the jump seat flipping through a *People* magazine when he appeared. I asked if I could get him anything and he didn't answer, but just glared at me.

"Why haven't you called me?"

"Because I have been flying a lot. I don't only do these trips. I speak three languages, and I have to do international trips as well."

His face softened and he seemed satisfied with my answer. But I couldn't help but wonder why he would be upset.

Maybe I was wrong about him being different from the others. He was acting like I was supposed to pay attention to him.

I just saw him as another player. So, I asked him, "Why are you upset that I haven't called you? Remember I am just your flight attendant, not a friend."

He looked at me, trying to choose his words carefully.

"Suppose I want to hang out with you and get to know you better, is that wrong?"

I explained to him the policy of the company's Charter Agreement that we all had to sign. No fraternizing, no asking for autographs, no taking photos and the list of things we were prohibited to do.

"So, who would find out? If you don't say anything, I won't. This is just between us. I can't get you off my mind and I think about you all the time" he said.

I looked at him and smiled. "I have three days off next week, so I'll call you."

"Can we go out to dinner or have drinks?" UH,

OH, I said in my mind. Not again!

He said his chef would prepare something special. I

said, "Okay then. I will call you."

Our affair was a well-kept secret, until it wasn't. Freaky moments in private hotel rooms, whispers to each other under the hum of engines, touches when nobody was looking.

For five years, Patrick and I lived in our own little bubble, believing no one knew.

But how wrong we were.

One night, after a heated win, we let our guard down.

Another player came to the back of the galley and caught us kissing.

I'll never forget the look in his eyes, part shock, part amusement, part danger.

Within days, the rumors spread through the team like wildfire. And then, the hammer dropped.

His management pulled him into a closed-door meeting. The message was clear: clean up your image, or kiss your endorsements goodbye.

The next thing I knew, he was engaged to a woman, a total stranger. He called me one last time, his voice was heavy with regret. "I had no choice," he said. "They own me."

And just like that, five years of lustful moments evaporated into thin air. Luckily for me, this didn't escalate to the drama that happened years ago.

No press, and no airline management involved. I

vowed from that day... no more athletes!

Would I live up to this promise to myself? That remained to be seen. When my heart was involved, I tended to fall for the same crap, but in order to get a different result I had to change my thoughts. I had to recognize the red flags. I had to acknowledge my triggers. I liked what I liked and loved what I loved.

Unfortunately, navigating a love life or lack thereof didn't come with a manual or a self-help book.

Falling in love for Dummies.

I seemed to read that book regularly...

63
Duty and Sacrifice

DOING CHARTER FLIGHTS DIDN'T JUST INCLUDE athletes. We flew many different types of passengers. Military, White House Press Corps, and other elite clientele. Flying with professional athletes was intense. Flying with soldiers was another story. Those weren't men drenched in wealth and fame.

They were kids, barely old enough to drink, heading off to war zones with uncertain futures. The mood was different.

Some drank too much, trying to numb the fear of flying. Others sat quietly, staring out the window, gripping the armrests like they could hold on to life itself.

I could remember most of them asking for cans of Coke. I later found out that a can of Coke made them feel like being back at home.

Then there were the flights back abroad. And many of them never made it back home. I'd never forget the sorrow in the air on those flights. The way their brothers sat in grief, staring at the empty seats where their friends should have been deeply pained me inside.

I, too, know about loss.

The way some of them wept, others stone-faced, carrying the kind of grief no one should have to bear tore my soul apart. I hated flying Military charters. Those were the worst trips I had to do, and I tried hard to avoid them.

The White House press corps, on the other hand, was a different ballgame, and they had home court advantage. The reporters held secrets the world wasn't ready for, secrets that could get you killed.

I overheard conversations that could have changed elections, ended careers, even toppled governments. They whispered about affairs in the Oval Office, scandals waiting to explode, and stories they had to sit on, at least for the moment.

I knew things before they made the national headlines. And I knew the price of that knowledge was silence.

64

Meeting The Legendary Congressman

DURING THE TIMES WHEN I WASN'T DOING charter flights, I had to return to doing regular domestic and international trips. There were so many adventurous and memorable trips that I could talk about, but those were just a few of my all-time favorites.

The flight was supposed to be easy. Five empty seats in First Class. It was an unexpected gift that promised a peaceful day in the sky. I was already imagining how smooth the service would be, how I might even catch my breath between sips of coffee and Bailey's

Irish cream and/or a gin and tonic.

About fifteen minutes before departure, the gate agent came rushing down the jet bridge.

Short of breath, her eyes were wide. "We're holding the flight," she said. "Five First Class VIPs are boarding."

In my mind, I muttered, *oh shit*. VIPs came with conditions. It meant all eyes would be on everything. The scrutiny and the pressure I didn't feel like dealing with.

"Who is it?" I asked.

"Politicians," she replied, vague as a foghorn. I walked into the cockpit to alert the pilots. I gave them a heads-up that the easy part of our day we thought we had just flown out the window.

Five minutes before departure, the jet bridge trembled. The door opened, and in they came. Five dignified men clad in dark suits. Their presence was undeniable. But it was him who stole all the air from the room.

Congressman John Lewis.

He was a living legend. A man who'd marched with Dr. King, bled on the Edmund Pettus Bridge, and carried the weight of freedom on his back for decades. He was dashing and debonair.

I had admired him from afar, read his words, seen him on television, and heard his speeches.

And now he was standing just feet from me, trying to coordinate seats with his team.

In my awe, I forgot to close the First Class curtain, and that moment became something else entirely. Passengers in the main cabin who were wondering why we were delayed had seen him and the flight erupted.

People began to clap. One by one, the entire aircraft rose to their feet in applause.

Congressman Lewis, with his quiet grace, walked to the front of the main cabin, placed his hand over his heart, and nodded in gratitude. He didn't speak. He didn't need to.

Back in his seat, I leaned in gently. "Would you care for something to drink, sir?"

"Water," he said, softly. His eyes still glowed from being exalted.

He was having an intense discussion with the other men. I didn't want to interrupt, but duty called.

"Excuse me, gentlemen," I said, "sorry to intrude, but if you need anything (coffee, snacks) please let me know. I am Kurt, and I am your lead flight attendant who will be taking care of you."

His aides asked for coffee. Congressman Lewis asked again, simply, for water.

As I handed him his glass, he looked at me curiously. "Jamaican?"

I smiled. "Yes. How did you know?"

"Your voice over the announcements. I thought to myself he must be from Trinidad or maybe Jamaica."

We both laughed. We talked a little more. I told him about the time I studied in Paris, and stories about the skies we both travelled through on an aircraft.

He was kind, warm, curious. A lion with velvet paws. He said I looked like a young Johnny Mathis, and I told him that I had been told that many times.

I did a few lines from one of his songs entitled "Chances Are, For I Wear A Silly Grin" and he laughed and clapped.

As we began our descent, he reached into his jacket and handed me his personal business card. Not the one with the congressional seal; it was the card with his private number.

I never did call him. Not because I didn't want to, but because I didn't know what to do with something so sacred.

What could I say to a man like that? That I was just a flight attendant, a boy from Jamaica who'd somehow found himself sharing air with legends?

About three months later, Delta Airlines selected a few of us to attend the GLAAD Awards. It was a black-tie event with expensive champagne and the flashing lights of the media. I spotted him across the room, and it took my breath away.

He was surrounded, of course by his entourage. Everyone wanted a piece of him. But eventually, he crossed the ballroom and stood in front of me. He tilted his head slightly, searching my face.

"The Jamaican flight attendant, Johnny Mathis" I said.

His eyes lit up. "Kirt," he said, wrapping me in a hug. "Why haven't you call me?"

I made up a lie. Something about flying too much, international trips, back-to-back trips. The truth was, I didn't feel worthy.

The press took photos of us. Our arms were around each other's waist. When he left, he touched my elbow and said, "Stop by my table." And I did.

Two months later, there was another gala at the HRC. Then came another with CNN reporter Don Lemon.

We kept bumping into each other like fate was trying to speak. Eventually, I found the courage to call his number. He answered on the first ring, and we spoke. He couldn't talk for long because he had a meeting in ten minutes.

Then one day, his voice came through the phone like a quiet

drumroll. "Hello Kirt. It's John Lewis. I was wondering," he said, casual as a whisper, "would you like to have dinner at the White House with President Barack and Mrs. Obama?"

I was silent. Not because I didn't hear him, but because my heart had suddenly left my body. He chuckled, sensing my shock.

"I'm serious," he said. "Break out the black-tie."

I said yes and we made the necessary arrangements. I flew to D.C. and stayed at the Ritz Carlton Hotel, located close to the White House. The room was already paid for.

Then the desk clerk handed me an envelope and when I went to the suite, I opened it and read the contents.

"Be ready by 7pm. In the lobby, my chauffeur will be waiting for you. He will be wearing white gloves."

I sat on the bed in the hotel room and thought about all the black-tie events I had seen him at.

Could he have been observing me all this time. Seeing how I carried myself gracefully?"

The thought crossed my mind.

65

Someone Worth Knowing

THE NIGHT OF THE DINNER, THE AIR IN WASHINGTON, D.C., tingles ran up my spine. The anticipation was electric and sacred.

It had the kind of energy that only came when you brushed up against history.

The motorcade took us safely to the gates. I'll never forget the moment I stepped into the White House, not as a tourist, but as a guest. A marine opened the grand doors, and a butler escorted us into the reception room.

There was champagne on silver trays, soft music playing in the background, and a crowd full of senators, ambassadors, journalists, and changemakers. And yet Congressman Lewis was the one who made me feel like royalty.

Congressman Lewis came over, took my hand, and said, "You look radiant." Just like that. No fuss. No flirt. You're the truth."

Then the moment came. The Obamas entered the room like

royalty in motion. Barack was tall, graceful, and warm; Michelle was radiant, commanding, and regal.

And somehow, Congressman Lewis introduced me to them like I was someone worth knowing. "This is my friend," he said fondly. "He's very special. He's my Delta Airlines flight attendant."

The President shook my hand and smiled. "So, you're the one who keeps him grounded," he joked. Mrs. Obama, with her soft but knowing gaze, said, "It's always the ones behind the scenes who hold everything together."

That was a very weird and awkward introduction I said to myself, and I wasn't sure what the President and Mrs. Obama interpreted it as, or what they meant.

Dinner was served in the State Dining Room under the gaze of Abraham Lincoln's portrait. Candlelight flickered off the crystal glasses, and conversation flowed like aged wine. I sat two seats away from the President. I barely touched my food. I was too enchanted by every word, every laugh, every historic breath in that room.

At one point, John leaned over and said, "I told you that you'd belong here."

And at that moment, I believed him. I wasn't a guest because of luck. I was there because someone who had walked through fire saw me. I wasn't just as a flight attendant or a handsome face in a ballroom. I was also as a young man worthy of history's embrace.

That night, I shook hands with senators, whispered greetings to diplomats, and laughed with people whose names were printed in headlines. Spoke to the Spanish ambassador in Spanish and the French foreign minister who I told that I studied at the Sorbonne was a treasure.

I held my own talking about politics. I shared my views on climate change. I felt like I was being tested, and I passed with flying colors.

But I only remembered him. I remembered the way he watched me and smiled. He was proud. Not of what I looked like, but of how far I'd come.

Congressman Lewis and I kept in touch. He was never inappropriate. He was always respectful. But there was something in the way he saw me.

It was something more than just admiration. Something unspoken. I loved him very much. Quietly. Deeply. And maybe that was enough.

When he passed away in 2020, I cried in the galley. I didn't even make it home before the sobs started. I couldn't go to the funeral. I was in Tokyo, Japan on a trip. I think it was best that I hadn't gone. Maybe grief was heavier when you've held hands with history.

But I still have that card. I still remembered that moment on the plane when the world stood up for a man who never stopped standing up for them.

And I, a guy from Jamaica who studied in Paris and served coffee in the clouds, got to sit beside him.

If only for a little while.

There was a reason people love a good conspiracy theory. The truth was that the world thrived on secrets.

And I was the invisible observer, the guy who saw it all but never said a word.

Until now.

66

The Freak-Offs

FOR YEARS, I TRANSPORTED MILLIONS OF DOLLARS' worth of goods across the world. I kept my head down, my mouth shut, and my hands steady. Until that day I realized I was carrying something much more dangerous than jewels. It wasn't a package. It was a secret. A secret so explosive that, if exposed, it could take down one of the most powerful men in the world.

I understood I wasn't just playing a game. I was part of it. I did this for over five years when Pan Am went into bankruptcy, and I changed airlines.

Looking back, my career wasn't just about flying. It was about navigating power, temptation, and danger. The skies held stories no one would ever believe.

But now, for the first time, I was telling them.

On one occasion, one of my flying partners, Percy, who was very well connected, asked if I wanted to go with him to a party and if I had something white to wear. I told him I had my white uniform short sleeve shirt, and he had a pair of white shorts that fit me perfectly.

I always traveled with white sneakers. Well, it so happened, it was one of those parties you heard about, but you had to see it to believe it. Our phones were taken away from us at the door and we were driven to a dock where a yacht awaited us stocked with Ciroc liquor, bottles of baby oil and food galore.

I didn't have to name the host but the word "freak-off" may give you a hint. It was wild and everybody who was anybody was there. It was a real eye-opener, and I saw and heard things that I wish I hadn't. The all-white party made me realize that celebrities were no better than us common folks.

They just had money, and didn't know what to do with it. If I started naming names of some of the well-known folks, your jaws would drop open.

But that wasn't my only eye-opening party.

There were parties. And then there were *those* parties. The kind that regular people whispered about in crew lounges and luxury hotel hallways.

The kind where your phone is taken at the door, and you sign your name on an NDA before you even hear the bass drop.

I was young. Fresh into the industry. Wide-eyed but not stupid. I had seen glamour, but this was something else entirely.

The gateway drug wasn't cocaine. It was access. And the man who opened that door for me was Percy.

Percy had been flying for over a decade. He was a tall, sharp-tongued, impossibly well-groomed veteran of the skies. He wore his uniform like a Tom Ford suit and knew everyone. He'd flown with rock stars, diplomats, and oil barons.

His real connections came alive when we touched down in cities like LA, New York, Miami, or even Berlin. One night, out of the blue, he turned to me and said, "You're coming with me. But be cool, understand? No phones. No questions."

We pulled up to a Spanish-style mansion tucked in the Hollywood Hills. Black Range Rovers lined the street. Inside, there was no red carpet, this was the real A-list. The kind of people who were the stories, not the ones chasing them.

At the entrance, a well-dressed man in sunglasses (at night?) took my phone.

He slid an NDA across a marble-topped table. I hesitated long enough to wonder if I was in over my head, then I signed.

The moment I stepped in, it felt like I'd entered a parallel universe.

Crystal chandeliers reflected off designer sunglasses. Tables were littered with everything from Dom Pérignon to diamonds, and little bowls filled with party favors that weren't exactly candy. Cocaine wasn't just offered, it was expected. MDMA and GHB floated through the room like perfume. Everyone was either high, horny, or hiding something.

And in the middle of it all, there he was: Luther Vandross.

I knew his voice long before I knew his face. But here, there was no soft ballad or shy smile. He was electric. Louder. Free. Draped in a silk shirt that clung to his body, laughing with two younger men who looked like they had walked off a Calvin Klein billboard.

Openly, they touched him, affectionately, playfully. And he welcomed it.

"You never saw him like this on stage," Percy murmured in my ear, eyes scanning the room. "But this is the real Luther. This is where he breathes."

And it wasn't just him.

There was a Grammy-winning rapper in a corner booth, grinding against a male dancer with gold glitter on his chest. A Hollywood action hero (married with kids) was in the pool, drunk and sloppy, with his arm wrapped around a drag queen dressed like Marilyn Monroe.

I saw a famous late-night host doing lines off cocaine off a glass table, right next to a sitcom star who'd built an entire career on being the wholesome dad-next-door.

They were all There, away from the cameras, the contracts, and the charades.

That night ended with me in a hot tub, sipping something I couldn't name, while an Oscar-nominated actress whispered into my ear, "You're cute... but you're new. Don't ever get caught talking about this. They will end you."

She wasn't joking. Those parties weren't just for pleasure. They were playgrounds for the powerful.

But they came with silent rules, guarded by NDAs and reinforced by fear.

I knew flight attendants who had been blacklisted just for name-dropping the wrong celebrity in a hotel lobby.

And yet... I kept going.

Percy brought me again and again. Vegas, NYC lofts, yacht parties off the coast of Greece. And with every encounter, I saw more. Learned more.

Things that never made it to the tabloids. I

kept their secrets. Until now.

Because the truth was, while they were hiding behind masks, I was discovering myself. It wasn't about sex or drugs or fame. It was about power.

And I had just started to realize that maybe... I had some too.

67

Basketball Jones

ANOTHER MAJOR ENCOUNTER I HAD WAS WITH an author I had heard about but had never met. He was on a flight from Detroit to Atlanta and I was working in the main cabin. Marc Sanders, our Lead Flight Attendant, rushed down from the first class cabin to tell me that an author named E. Lynn Harris was onboard and wanted to see me.

I asked him why he would want to talk to me and Marc confessed that he had struck up a conversation with Mr. Harris and told him I flew for the NBA and that I had dated a player years ago. I was livid.

Only a handful of people knew this and without asking me, Marc had broken my trust. So, I told him I wasn't interested in meeting anyone.

However, the sneaky son-of-a-bitch brought this man down to the main cabin galley to meet me. I gave Marc a dirty look of which Mr. Harris saw, and he begged me not to take it out on

Marc, because he had heard so much about me that I peeked his interest.

He would love to talk to me if that was possible and gave me his card. I told him I would think about it. I did end up calling him and we planned a meeting at his home in Atlanta.

Coincidentally, he was throwing a party that weekend, so I saw an all-male group which included famous rappers, athletes, actors, producers, television personalities and pretty much the black who's who elite of Atlanta all dressed in white.

I hadn't planned on staying over but he convinced me to spend the night in one of his six guest bedrooms. The next morning, his butler prepared breakfast and that was when we began talking in depth about my relationship with John.

He did ask my permission to record it, and I agreed.

I told him about how we met, the lifestyle, the five years of rich lifestyle, us traveling on my Pan Am employee companion passes first class around the world.

I also told him about his best friend getting jealous and he told the NBA league management of our affair.

The league gave John an ultimatum to get married and I was removed from the Pan Am Charter squad. So, having told Lynn all the story he said he thought it would be a great book.

About three months later, I got a call from Lynn asking if I could come to Atlanta. When I arrived, he handed me a script entitled "Basketball Jones."

Although I really didn't feel like reading a book, once I started, I couldn't stop. It was genius. He had changed it up and switched some things around. When I finished, I gave him a big hug. What a genius.

As payment for the story, he quit-claimed an apartment in Midtown Atlanta over to me and $10K cash.

Unfortunately, this would turn out to be his last book and last best seller. He passed away while doing a promotional tour for *Basketball Jones*.

He was such a genius that the word JONES spells out the name indirectly of the NBA basketball player I dated for eight years.

But the wildest of my flights was getting drunk with Miss L'Oreal who was then married to Tony Parker, who played for the San Antonio Spurs.

She came prepared on the flight with her own drinks and boy we did have fun.

She said she just wanted a "smidge," and I said I should just try it and tell her how I liked it.

I reminded her that I was on duty, and she begged me, "PLEASE,"... and who could resist her.

Boy, that tequila was good, it was called CASA DEL SOL TEQUILA and later we took a photograph together and you could tell thar I looked drunk in my uniform standing beside her smiling like I had won a million dollars.

68
The End Of An Era

IT WAS TIME. TIME FOR ME TO SAY GOODBYE to the airlines. After thirty-years, I had to say goodbye. I was tired and this routine had become old. What was there left to see? I had gone through two bankruptcies, and a merger. I had been to over 100 countries in my thirty-two years of flying.

My first trip that I ever worked was New York (JFK) to Rome, Italy in December 1982 with Pan Am. So, I promised myself that my very first trip was to Rome with Pan Am, so why not end my very last trip to Rome with Delta Airline....and that was exactly what I did.

I traded a trip with another flight attendant just so I could do my final trip to Rome, Italy.

All the crew members knew this was my final farewell and they treated me so well, they put me up in First Class to work and I had a ball. I never slept the whole night.

When I landed, I changed into my jeans and a nice shirt, and ventured off everywhere. I finished at the Vatican late at night at 9 p.m., knowing we had to be up at 7am for the van to take us back to the airport for our return flight back to the USA.

The return flight was a blast. We had some leftover caviar and champagne, and we were drinking after service. An hour before we landed, Antonio, our Purser, told the passengers on the P.A. system that I was retiring after thirty plus years of flying and this flight was my last flight.

The applause was overwhelming. I felt like Miss America, making my way down the aisle of the 747 aircraft thanking everyone who were standing and applauding. My hand over my heart and bowing as I made my way to the back.

As I reached the back of the aircraft, one of the flight attendants told me that the Captain needed to see me in the cockpit. I figured he probably heard the applause and also wanted to congratulate me as well.

Instead, he handed me an ACARS note which said I would be drug tested as soon as I landed back in the USA.

We had all heard the dirty rumors that the company didn't want to pay out benefits to folks who were retiring so they were trying everything to get you fired. I ran down to the back galley and showed the crew the ACARS message and we went to work.

Four cups of black coffee, two gallons of water, tonic water, sparkling water, ginger ale, cranberry juice and more black coffee. I drank so much that I felt bloated and wanted to throw up which I did, and did another round of water.

Upon arrival, I was met by two drug testers, and I prayed for three days till I got my results that I tested negative and that I needed to come in and sign my benefits and travel pass forms.

And so ended my illustrious thirty-two years, four airlines, one hundred countries, seven continents, and now all I had were my memories.

Retirement was supposed to feel like exhaling after a long flight. When I finally touched down, I rested my wings. But six months in, I was floating aimlessly.

I had nowhere to be, no gate calls, no uniform, no first-class cabin. I went from jet-setting to grocery shopping, and on one unremarkable afternoon, Kroger's became my unexpected terminal for takeoff into a brand-new chapter.

I was just browsing, looking over the price for milk, eggs, and a few vegetables, when I noticed her smile. She was polished, confident, warm.

We passed each other once, twice, and again in the frozen food aisle. There was something familiar about her. Then she stopped and said with a tilt of her head, "Did you work for Pan

Am Airlines?"

I froze. My hand lingered over a pack of frozen shrimp.

"I used to. I was a flight attendant, but I left Pan Am in 1991 when they went bankrupt and ended up at Delta. I retired six months ago after thirty-two years of flying."

She smiled, brighter now. "I knew I remembered you."

You'd swear I was a cow staring at a new fence because I had no idea who she was.

69

Aisle 15 At Kroeger's

SHE ASKED IF I REMEMBERED HER AND her husband sitting in First Class, seats 2A and 2C. A flicker of memory sparked. Then she said, "It was the day you lost your balance coming down the aisle with champagne." Her husband, she reminded me, had jumped up to help gather the broken glass.

That was when it all rushed back.

Mrs. McIntyre in 2A. And her husband, tall and gracious, was always watching out for her. That flight, over sixty years ago, was the one right after I had returned from burying my grandmother in Jamaica.

I was emotionally gutted, but I insisted on working. The Lead Flight Attendant had told the first class cabin that I wouldn't be finishing the service, but I never knew they explained why.

She looked me in the eyes and said, "We all knew something had happened. Then she told us about your grandmother. We were heartbroken for you."

My chest tightened. "All twenty-six passengers in First Class told the Lead to send you our love and prayers," she continued.

I didn't know what to say. I had walked up and down that aisle thinking no one noticed my hands trembling or the red in my eyes. Yet here was a woman who carried my grief in her heart since 1987, and still remembered.

She asked me what I'd been doing since retiring, and I told her the truth. I was relaxing, trying to figure out what came next.

Then she dropped the kind of line that could only be fate. "Well... I'm the general manager of the Marriott Marquis Hotel in Atlanta. I would love for you to come work for me, Kirt."

I blinked. She handed me her card as if it was a golden ticket. "Think about it," she said, with the calm authority of someone who knew the answer was already yes.

I did think about it. For three whole weeks. And then I called.

70
The Ambassador of Atlanta

THE MARRIOTT MARQUIS IN ATLANTA WAS a skyscraping hive of luxury, energy, and constant motion. It was the largest hotel in the city. There were over fifteen-hundred rooms, an iconic atrium that spirals into the heavens, and a guest list that read like the Forbes 500. My new title? Ambassador. It sounded vague, but it was glamorous and ambiguous.

What did it mean? Everything. I became the soul of the lobby. The hand that welcomed guests, the smile that reassured the wealthy, the memory that recalled not just names, but preferences. I was part concierge, part diplomat, part storyteller.

And I was good at it. I knew how to read body language from a thousand feet in the air, how to handle stress with poise, how to remember names and cocktail orders, and how to handle personalities from celebrities to senators.

The skills I learned from the airline translated effortlessly into my new position. The hotel became my new terminal. And then came the global convention. Four hundred managers from every corner of Marriott International descended on Atlanta, including the crown jewel: The Ritz - Carlton. For one week, I had my chance to shine, handling everything from meet-and-greets to high-profile requests.

That's when I met him, the manager of the Ritz - Carlton Fort Lauderdale. Sharp suit. Sharper eyes.

"You're from Fort Lauderdale I'm told?"

"I split my time between there and Atlanta," I said. "Would you ever consider working at the Ritz - Carlton?"

I laughed. "I just got here a year ago. I don't think they'll let me go."

He smiled, a quiet confidence behind his words. "Leave that to me." And just like that, within weeks, I was walking through the private glass doors of the Ritz - Carlton Fort Lauderdale as their newest VIP Club Lounge Concierge.

71

The Velvet Cage

THE CLUB LOUNGE WASN'T JUST EXCLUSIVE, it was my sacred ground. Reserved for the elite of the elite: millionaires, investment titans, and celebrities who wanted luxury without the spotlight.

I was their guardian angel in pressed black slacks and a silk tie. I handled everything. Limousines. Broadway tickets.

Dry cleaning for their tuxedos. Private wine tastings. And the drinks, oh, the drinks were fabulous!

I brought my airline bar skills to new heights, mixing Manhattans, martinis, and mojitos with flair and flourish. My signature? A custom ginger-lime martini that guests started requesting by name.

There were perks. Mr. Van Dunn, an investment broker from New York, tipped me one-hundred dollars every visit. He came every weekend like clockwork.

There were whispered conversations, stories swapped over midnight cigars, and quiet nods of respect that said: You belong here.

But the Ritz was a different kind of pressure.

Unlike the airline, where passengers disappeared after a few hours, hotel guests stayed. Days. Weeks. You were theirs. Their fixer, their go-to, their butler, their therapist.

There were no layovers, no hotel rooms for you to escape to. Just round-the-clock demands with luxury smiles.

I did it for a year and a half. Then I stepped away but not for the reason you might think.

Because life had other plans.

My next chapter...was tragedy.

72

The High Life and the Dark Corners

IN THE MIDST OF THIS NEW LIFE, I MET HIM. A charming man with an allure I couldn't resist. I knew that his faced looked familiar, but I just couldn't remember. Finally, he said hello and called me by a nickname only few people knew. I did have my Ritz - Carlton name tag on my uniform, so why did he call me "Skygod."

I looked at him for a while. "Kirt the Flirt," he said while handing me his business card.

It was my old friend Brian from my Pan Am days. We went back almost twenty years. What was he doing there in the VIP lounge? The Rolex and diamond bracelet said it all. We reconnected. He had gotten bigger, with grey hair on the sides.

There was something odd about him and you could tell something was wrong with him. This was not the Brian of twenty years ago.

We talked for quite a bit, and he called up old friends on his cell who I hadn't heard from in years.

We went out several times after that, but I sensed something was wrong. He drank a lot and always smelled like he was smoking weed.

I tried to avoid him after that, but by him knowing where to find me at the Ritz - Carlton, I really couldn't escape him.

I hadn't heard from him in weeks. Mysteriously, he had stopped coming by the hotel. A few months after our reunion, I got a call from a mutual friend who told me that I needed to go over and check on Brian because he was out of control.

I agreed, since I knew where he lived, and said I would check up on him the next day. It was my day off, so I got there around 1:30pm and went to the door which was slightly open.

I rang the doorbell anyway and entered. Hoping to see Brian, instead, I walked into a nightmare.

He was on the floor, dead.

73
Tax Office

A HEROIN OVERDOSE HAD CLAIMED BRIAN'S LIFE. How did I know? You could see the white foam at the corner of his mouth.

I was devastated, but soon, grief gave way to survival instincts. I called 9-1-1.

During the questioning from the police, the president of his condo association let it be known that he was behind on his association fees.

They had started proceedings with legal actions to put a lien on his condo.

I knew he didn't have a Will and no next of kin, at least that's what I believed.

His apartment was behind on condo fees and taxes. It was a ticking time bomb of financial ruin.

Desperation clouded my judgment, and in a moment of reckless calculation, I asked myself what if I get the property in my name.

The idea sounded good at the time, so a few days later, I

forged his name on a quit-claim deed, got a friend who was a notary to notarize it and then filed it with the tax office.

The property was now mine, or so I thought. But

fate had other plans.

74

The Arrest and the Truth Unveiled

THE KNOCK ON MY DOOR CAME A WEEK LATER. His two brothers had surfaced, and they were furious. I had no idea Brian had any family. For the twenty years I had known him, he never mentioned having siblings. They discovered what I had done, and the authorities were called.

My arrest was swift and unforgiving.

The charges were stacked against me. Grand theft, falsifying paperwork, forging a deceased person's name, and larceny. But the worst was yet to come.

Fingerprints. A routine procedure that unraveled fifteen years of careful deception. When they ran my prints, the system spat out a different name. It was the name I had used for the airline for thirty years.

The confusion led to a deeper investigation, and soon, my secret life was laid bare.

Not one, but two legal aliases, three different passports, two different social security numbers, and they were all legitimate.

The discovery sent shockwaves through the authorities.

Who was I really?

They suspected espionage, especially when they uncovered my Jamaican passport.

The situation escalated. The government deemed me a flight risk, and deportation loomed over me like a guillotine.

My past, once my shield, had now become my prison.

But there was still a way out, a final gambit that could change everything.

75

Prison and the Fight for Asylum

MY LAWYER, A SKILLED NEGOTIATOR, STRUCK a deal with the district attorney. Instead of deportation, I would serve eighteen months in federal prison. This was not mercy, maybe it was strategy. He knew what awaited me in Jamaica.

The intense homophobia in my homeland was not just a social inconvenience; it was a death sentence.

Seeking asylum became my lifeline.

Federal prison was an entirely different world, one that operated by its own set of rules.

Here, survival wasn't about skill or intelligence, it was about adaptation.

I watched and learned. The hierarchy, the barter system, the unspoken alliances. It was a game, a brutal one, and I was determined to play it well.

Through it all, I began to see the prison system for what it really was. It was a machine that thrived on broken lives. It was not just about punishment; it was about control, about keeping people in cycles they could rarely escape.

And yet, in the midst of it all, I found something unexpected. Clarity.

For the first time in years, I was truly myself. No

aliases, no forged documents, just me.

However, one night I found out the hard way that the softest or non-hardcore men were targets. I became a victim of that cold, cruel world.

I couldn't report anything, or I would be labeled a snitch. So, for three whole weeks I never slept. Always in fear that those three black guys would come again. I was released three months after that.

The question now was, what would I do with this second chance?

76

Betrayed by Blood

OVER THE YEARS, I HAD INVESTED IN PROPERTY and owned two homes. One was in Midtown Atlanta, which E. Lynn Harris gave me and was an exclusive high-rise on the 27th floor that overlooked downtown. The view was breathtaking. The other was a three-bedroom condo in Fort Lauderdale, my primary residence, filled with antiques from my grandmother's estate.

Both were mortgage-free, symbols of my hard work and success. But being in prison meant I couldn't pay bills, including the homeowners' association fees. Michelle's son, my nephew Lloyd, who had visited me weekly, seemed like the only person I could trust. So, I made what would be the biggest mistake of my life.

I assigned him Power of Attorney to handle my affairs.

Lloyd had a criminal past, but I believed in him. I had been his only uncle, the one he always turned to when he and his mother, Michelle, were at odds, especially when she found out that he was gay.

Four months later, I called Simone from prison. She asked why I had sold my apartment and not tell her. Confused, I told her I hadn't, but she insisted it had been sold, and movers were emptying it out.

When she confronted Lloyd, he claimed I had given him permission to sell both properties.

My heart sank.

Everything I had built was slipping away. Lloyd had lied to everyone. He sold my homes, my furniture, my antiques, everything worth over half a million dollars was gone.

I called my sister for answers, only to be met with cold indifference. She told me I was a fool for trusting Lloyd and that it was my own fault. Later, I discovered she was the mastermind behind the scheme.

With the money, Lloyd bought a Maserati, expensive jewelry, and a $150,000 home in North Carolina.

Paid in full.

My own sister, Michelle, took a hefty cut of the spoils.

When I consulted my lawyer, his words crushed me. "You gave him absolute Power of Attorney. There's nothing we can do." My life savings, my investments, my cars—everything was gone.

77
Homeless and Hopeless

AFTER MY RELEASE, I HAD NOWHERE TO GO. I was homeless, abandoned by my own family. I had worked hard for everything, and in an instant, it had all vanished.

A case manager referred me to a shelter, but I was only allowed to stay for six months.

Panic set in.

The only clothes I had were the ones I had been arrested in eighteen months prior.

The shelter provided me with used clothes, and I was assigned to a roommate.

He was a former prisoner battling PTSD, a condition I would later be diagnosed with myself.

Rebuilding my life was an uphill battle. Lloyd had used my ID fraudulently, and my driver's license was flagged.

My credit was destroyed, maxed-out cards and debts that weren't mine haunted me.

Depression consumed me. I was withdrawn into myself. I

didn't trust anyone or anything. I was at my wits end. My family betrayed me and took all of my money and my valuables behind my back while pretending t be there for me at my lowest.

I had nothing else to lose, or nothing left to give.

My tears were endless.

On January 1, 2022, New Years Day, my 60th birthday, I tried to take my own life.

78

The Accident and Loss of Leni

AFTER MY FAILED SUICIDE ATTEMPT, I FOUND myself adrift, cut off from the world. My phone was gone, and I had lost touch with friends and family, leaving me desperate for connection. In that bleak moment, I turned to Facebook and Instagram, searching for familiar faces.

That's when I found Leni, an ex-lover from years past.

He was married now, but when I revealed my situation

(homeless, living in a shelter, struggling to survive) he didn't hesitate. He promised to come to see me that weekend.

True to his words, Leni came and picked me up that Saturday evening. For the first time in months, I felt a flicker of normalcy. We headed to Outback Steakhouse, where laughter and shared memories flowed as easily as the drinks.

It was as if the years between us had melted away, and for a fleeting moment, I allowed myself to believe that maybe things were getting better.

The accident had started as a golden hour ride. The windows down, laughter swirling through the car like wind chimes on a summer breeze.

Somewhere between memory and destination, we had shared stories under the soft glow of the setting sun, believing for a moment that life could still be beautiful.

But then there was the sound of metal screaming, a guttural crunch that felt unreal. A heartbeat of silence, then chaos. My world turned upside down. Glass exploded around me like frozen fireworks. The road vanished beneath us, swallowing us whole.

On the way back to the shelter, a car barreled through a red light, slamming into the passenger side where I sat. In an instant, the world turned to darkness.

When I regained consciousness, I was in a hospital bed, disoriented and surrounded by the beeping of monitors and the concerned faces of two nurses. Pain surged through my lower back and leg like a wildfire, and I tried to move, but agony shot through me. I asked them what had happened, and one nurse gently informed me that I had suffered a fractured hip. Soon, the doctor was coming to explain my injuries, and the repercussions as well.

In that moment of confusion, my thoughts immediately turned to Leni. I asked about him, expecting to hear that he was in another room, recovering from minor injuries. The nurses exchanged glances, their silence heavy with unspoken words, before one finally said, "The doctor will be in to talk to you."

A few moments later, the doctor arrived, his face grave. He explained the severity of my injury, mentioning the possibility of a hip replacement. I barely registered his words, my mind racing elsewhere. I asked again about Leni, my heart pounding with hope.

The doctor hesitated, then exhaled slowly, delivering the news that shattered my world. "I'm so sorry. Leni didn't make it. He died at the scene."

I froze. My breath caught in my throat; I wanted to cry and scream out his name, but nothing came. Instead, an overwhelming pressure filled my chest, my heart pounding against my ribs.

The doctor must have noticed the change in my vitals because he quickly instructed the nurse to administer something. A moment later, everything blurred, and I was pulled into a deep, medicated sleep, the weight of grief too heavy to bear.

I spent a week in the hospital, trapped in a haze of pain and disbelief. Leni had been my lifeline in my darkest hour, and now, he was gone. Once again, I was alone. The accident took more than just Leni. It took everything.

In an instant, my world had shattered, and I was left to navigate the dark waters of grief and loss, forever changed. I didn't scream. I didn't cry. I just went numb.

Like someone had pulled the plug and let all the air out of me. The grief was too big to feel all at once. It came in waves, sometimes a sharp stab, sometimes just a heaviness in my chest like I'd swallowed a boulder whole.

But the accident didn't just take him. It took everything and now I had a broken hip, and couldn't walk.

The shelter director came to see me and assured me that I shouldn't worry about my accommodation and help would be provided once I was released.

He spoke to my physician privately about surgery and anticipated dates of discharge.

Surgery was postponed for reasons they called "systemic backlog" and "lack of insurance verification." Painkillers were rationed like wartime rations.

I shuffled through recovery like an aging veteran with a walker, each movement a battle. But even more brutal than the pain was what came after, and what *didn't* come back.

My property was gone. One in Atlanta, one in Fort Lauderdale. Eviction notices came like death certificates. Foreclosure documents came like tombstones. I tried to make calls. Plead. Reason. But once you were injured, uninsured, and alone, the world becomes a courtroom where you were always on trial and never get to testify.

Everything I'd built, all that I'd once called mine, slipped through my fingers like sand. I lost my homes, yes, but more than that, I lost my place in the world.

My sense of self, destroyed. My position, vindicated. My footing in a society that demands performance and punishes vulnerability was defunct.

I wasn't just broke. I was *broken*.

At first, I tried to keep up appearances. I told myself it was temporary. A setback, not a sentence. But over time, I became a ghost in my own life. I was a man moving through shadows of former glory, trying to survive in a reality that no longer recognized him.

From the outside, it looked like I was resting. Healing. But inside, I was unraveling.

My identity frayed at the edges. I was no longer "Kirt the businessman," or "Kirt the jet-setter," or "Kirt the charismatic presence in any room," or "Kirt the Flirt."

I was just a patient. A name on a chart. A man with a walker and nowhere to go. Grief didn't come with a roadmap. Trauma didn't ask for permission. And the fall from grace didn't give you a parachute.

All I had was pain, and time, and silence. And beneath that silence, something else began to grow. Not hope. Not yet.

But the seed of something harder. Sharper.

Something that refused to die.

79

Beneath the Surface of Despair

AFTER I WAS DISCHARGED FROM THE HOSPITAL, a well-seasoned nurse handed me a walker, and the staffing office ordered transportation to take me to the shelter.

But before we could depart, orders were given to the driver to take me a more handicap-friendly shelter with staff equipped to handle my mobility issues.

This new shelter had therapists on standby to give effective counsel to those who requested it.

I liked that, especially as I began to ascend from the ashes of betrayal. I stepped into a world that didn't care whether I limped, cried, or collapsed.

If my family could break my trust, then I wouldn't put anything past anyone. How could I trust anyone after dealing with the loss of everything I held dear, from my feelings, my body, my emotions, my finances and my material possessions, even my homes.

For the first time in my life, I was without an address. I didn't know which way was North, east, up, down left and right. Without direction, I should say. I walked on my self-esteem and my dignity like a red carpet event, only there were no lights and paparazzi snapping memorable photos.

God, where do I begin?

Reluctantly, the shelter became my sanctuary. A much-needed sabbatical.

The building was a repurposed warehouse located in the heart of the city that had forgotten how to make room for the broken.

During the entry process I was humiliated. The metal detectors made me feel like a peasant, when I was once a king in my own universe.

Flying all over the world, dining in hundreds of countries during my Sex and *the Aircraft* adventures with politicians, NBA players and distinguished gentlemen that was now urban legend amongst the flight attendant world, but now I was broke, broken and homeless.

The questioning glares made my skin crawl. Ugh, and the clipboard questionnaire I had to fill out with a pen that kept running out of ink felt like a government's version of soul extraction and I had nothing left to give.

"Any addictions? History of violence? HIV status?"

I was no longer Kirt. I was Case #11843. I had nothing! I was a man with a fractured hip, a walker that got on my last good nerve, and a luxurious past that was both a gift and a curse. I was assigned to a cot surrounded by men who spoke in code, who twitched in their sleep, and those who had cold eyes that made me shudder.

The next week, a tall, somewhat disgruntled man with dark eyes smeared feces across the bathroom walls. I wanted to throw up. And the smell was horrendous.

Another man with a tan complexion ridden with psoriasis screamed every damn night about voices taunting him. The shit drove me crazy.

The only thing was no one else could hear them. He got into a lot of arguments with other people, but it never escalated to anything.

Ignoring him, I applied for Medicaid. Three times. I was rejected every time.

The first time, I was missing documents, which was ridiculous because I submitted everything in a timely fashion.

The second time, my medical records were incomplete, which was complete bullshit because I kept regular doctor visits, and was caught up on immunizations since the day I boarded Pan

Am Airlines on my first day of employment.

I've flown all over the world. I had many passports and had to be immunized before I traveled to Africa, Greece or any other country around the world.

Try again. Medicaid. Then the third rejection was because...at that point I was deeply frustrated. Why was I continuously being rejected? I was already wallowing within the depths of my losses. I was crawling through the thorns of my suffering and pain. To give it a bureaucratic euphemism, *they don't care.*

My handicap worsened. My body seemed to be at war with itself to the point my walker no longer sufficed. My right leg buckled without warning. The pain became unbearable.

I cried myself to sleep from the unbearable pain. I didn't have a home, money or friends. I didn't have anyone to call to help me, let alone bail me out of the bottom of the totem pole.

Also, I needed surgery, but without Medicaid or a hospital that would take me pro bono, I was stuck in limbo. I started using a wheelchair, and it sucked, but at least I was artificially mobile. My hands did all the work.

To my dismay, a few weeks later I was transferred to a different shelter.

It was a notorious shelter in the homeless community.

There, drugs possessed nearly all of them.

They peddled drugs.

Meth and crack gave the place a predatory energy. I tried to keep my head down, but it was impossible from a wheelchair. I nearly lost my mind.

How was I reduced to the slums?

One night, I made the mistake of using the microwave before a man named Donnie, who considered it *his* after 8 p.m.

Red-eyed, he stood over me, puffed out his frail chest, and curled his hands into balled fists.

"You think you're better than us 'cause you talk like James Bond?" he accused.

What was this whack job talking about?

I took the walker from the back of my wheelchair and used it to stand up. "Find you somebody to play with, because I'm not in the mood to argue with a cluck!"

Lunging at me, he threw a sucker punch. Swiftly, I blocked his punch with my right forearm.

My walker tipped from my left-handed grasp. I fell to the side, cracking my ribs against a bunk frame.

The other men laughed, smoking weed and doing dope. The

staff was nowhere to be found.

Holding my chest, I wasn't just gasping from pain, but I was delirious because I could die on this dirty floor, and no one would notice until the smell gave me away.

80

The Unexpected Messenger

ONE BEAUTIFUL MORNING, MY SALVATION ARRIVED clad in a fancy pinstripe suit. I should have known that something was coming. I awakened from slumber happier than usual, because I'd grown accustomed to loss and sadness, even severe depression.

The shelter was abuzz with news of the mayor coming to visit us! I assumed that it was a Public Relations visit. A photo op with the homeless was always top priority around election time, and I'd seen enough of the political bait and switch bullshit to last me a lifetime.

I expected fake handshakes and empty promises during his visit. He would burst through the doors with his ass-kissing entourage of yes sir, no sir, minions, making a grand entrance and flash a fake ass smile while blowing smoke up our asses.

Then leave us choking on the exhaust of their departing vehicles after they get our votes.

We definitely would be in their rearview.

What I didn't expect was for him to stop—*really stop*—when

he saw me.

"Hello, sir, how are you?"

"I'm doing great, thanks for asking. Mind if I sit?" he asked, nodding his head towards me.

I looked him over without being rude. "Suit yourself," I replied, motioning toward the battered plastic chair across from me. He was dapper, to say the least. We stared into each other's eyes for a New York minute before he said anything further.

"What's your story, if you don't mind my asking."

I told him a rough chop version. Not all of it, just enough to paint the picture.

I had Jamaican roots, I was a former flight attendant, I was a Sorbonne University graduate, I spoke four languages, and I experienced tragedy and loss.

His eyes never left mine.

"You were a flight attendant?" he asked, clearly intrigued.

"I was first class international. I knew the difference between a Sauvignon Blanc and a Chardonnay before most people knew what a passport was."

He chuckled. "I like your style."

We didn't formally introduce ourselves. I didn't ask for his name, and he didn't ask for mine. As short as our encounter was,

I enjoyed his company.

The next week, I received a care package from someone. I opened it with a smile, and I saw lotion, cologne, protein bars, and socks. A week later, an envelope with cash arrived for me from a mysterious donor.

There wasn't a card or a note. I racked my brain like crazy, trying to figure out who would show me love like that, but my mind was shooting blanks and hitting nothing but my blood pressure.

I thanked Jesus for the blessing, and didn't question it again or try to figure it out. I was still trying to get my life back together and find something to live for.

Then God's blessings showered me until I was soaked and wet from His glory. My Medicaid was suddenly approved. My name was quietly added to a housing list I'd been told was closed.

A month later, my surgery was scheduled.

A private car picked me up instead of special services and transportation.

I no longer had to go to regular hospital visits and deal with any bias and bigotry.

I was assigned to an actual rehabilitation center that greeted me with fresh bedsheets on the most comfortable mattress ever, and real food that provided much needed sustenance.

For eight weeks, I healed beautifully.

Every Friday, flowers arrived for me. Someone was giving me my flowers when I didn't feel worthy of smelling the petals.

They were bright, elegant, and was always accompanied by a card that simply read:

"Keep going. – R."

I didn't need to ask who sent the flowers....

81

The Kiss

AFTER A SUCCESSFUL JOURNEY THROUGH REHABILITATION (And yes,

it was grueling at times, but well worth it), I was placed in

transitional housing. The horrors of the shelters were things of the

past, and I thanked God for it. It could have been much worse, but

within two months, I had a key.

To a real apartment. My own apartment!

Thank you, Jesus!

I fell to my knees and gave Him all the praise and the glory. I

couldn't believe it!

I was blessed with a one bedroom, fully furnished by an

organization the mayor contacted.

Everything was coordinated, bringing out the beauty of my

apartment. The ceramic dishes and the towels matched the curtains

that danced slightly every time to air-conditioner came on, set on

auto.

I cried harder when I stood on the threshold in my bedroom

and saw my cozy bed.

My own bed!

Not a cot, even though I was thankful for that cot. I found my dignity again.

It was mine for as long as I lived.

I invited the mayor over and it wasn't out of obligation, but rather, confusion.

I was delighted that he accepted, and I kept my mouth shut. I was an introvert as of late, so my business was more private than a nun's panties during communion.

After he knocked on my door, I opened it and smiled.

"Thanks for inviting me over, Kirt."

We embraced. He smelled like a scent of honey on the summer breeze. His cologne made me weak in the knees.

"Thanks for coming." I extended my hand. "Come inside, please."

I closed and locked the door.

"I love what you did to the place."

"It was already furnished, but I appreciate the acknowledgement."

We sat across from each other on my modest couch. The silence was heavier than the furniture.

"Why?" I asked. "Why me?"

He hesitated, then gazed at me with sincerity.

"You reminded me of who I used to be, before the cameras and the titles. I had a life before I took office, and getting there wasn't crystal stairs.

"You are extremely intelligent," he continued. "You are a light in this world. We all have a story to tell. You may feel discarded, but you are *not* broken."

I nodded.

Then, out of the blue, he leaned up to my quivering lips. The kiss was gentle. Lingering. I wasn't sure if it was an ending or a beginning.

And then he was gone.

But the weight of that moment stayed.

It wasn't just the kiss that had me floating on cloud nine, ten, eleven, twelve and thirteen.

It was more about his giving heart and his compassion that resurrected my drive to succeed.

I judged the book by its cover, initially, when he first visited and walked into my life.

He was living proof that even in my darkest hour, God sent an angel who wore a suit and didn't ask for wings.

I was truly thankful and grateful. Everything I have ever been through flashed before my eyes and the Book of Job filtered through my mind at warped speed.

God didn't close a door without opening another.

But He never promised that He'd open that door right away.

Sometimes you had to be humbled.

82

Songs of the Ones I Loved and Lost

I LOVED MUSIC. SOME OF MY FAVORITE TUNES became the soundtrack of my life. There were songs that stitched themselves into my memory, not because they were on the radio, but because they were playing in the background of my life when my heart was wide open, and when it was broken.

Some people remembered their lovers by photographs that provoked their hearts to anger and regret. I remembered them with music. Each man I've truly loved had a song forever tied to his name. And each one left a note in my soul, a mark on my path, and a lesson I didn't always understand at the time.

Alex came into my life like a soft breeze through a cracked window. He was gentle, consistent, and forthcoming. He was patient in ways I didn't deserve. He had a calming presence, like a lighthouse after dark that lit my safe path across troubled waters to the sandy shore.

His song was "Get Here" by Oleta Adams.

"You can reach me by railway; you can reach me by trailway..."

Alex didn't ask for much. He just wanted closeness and a strong connection. He would've traveled across the world just to see me smile. And I—scared, distracted, unready—kept him at a distance. I always promised him more than I could give. He waited for me, and I let him wait too long until he inevitably slipped away.

He deserved better than breadcrumbs anyway.

When that song played now, I didn't just think of him....I felt the ache of all the waiting he did in silence.

Oh, well. Then there was Rick, my forbidden one. He was handsome, passionate, engaging and intoxicating. We met when we weren't supposed to. He belonged to someone else. But we found our lustful bodies entangled and our secret evenings burned too brightly until it fizzled out.

His song was "Saving All My Love For You" by Whitney Houston. *"A few stolen moments is all that we share..."*

He believed in destiny. I believed in desire. And somewhere in between, we lost our footing. What we had was never meant to last, but it did leave a scar. A sweet one, and a bitter one.

Farouk was unlike anyone I had ever met. He was beautiful, cultured, and magnetic. He was Turkish-Egyptian, with eyes that held centuries of mystery and pain from his bloodline.

He taught me how to slow down. To breathe. To trust

something deeper than just physical attraction. His song was "Open My Heart" by Yolanda Adams.

"Alone in a room, it's just me and you..."

Farouk believed in God with a quiet conviction, and he prayed for me even when I didn't believe in myself. He wanted to give me forever, but I couldn't even give him tomorrow.

He said, "You think love is a fire, but it's a garden. It has to be nurtured."

I didn't listen. I was still chasing fireworks when I had a whole field blooming in front of me.

Now, every time Yolanda's voice fills the air, I closed my eyes and remembered the warmth of his kitchen in Istanbul, the softness of his voice, and the prayers he whispered for a future we'd never have.

And then there was Michael Huguley.

Oh, Michael...

His love was like poetry.

It was raw, deep, and soul-wrenching. He loved me in ways I didn't think I deserved. He saw past the armor and held the broken pieces of me as if they were gold.

His song was "The First Time Ever I Saw Your Face" by Roberta Flack.

"I thought the sun rose in your eyes..."

With him, love was eternal.

Or so I thought. We'd lie in bed, with the song playing low in the background, and he'd trace my jawline with his fingers, like he was memorizing me for a time when I wouldn't be there.

I knew he needed more than I could give. And when I left, I saw something in his eyes I'll never forget. I saw the devastation dressed in silence.

I didn't just break his heart; I shattered something sacred that balanced his sanity.

That song now? It guts me. Every damn time.

And finally, there was Kendrick. Kendrick was rhythm, intellect, and a complete fucking mystery. He had a way of walking into a room and making the world feel like jazz, improvised, unexpected, beautiful.

His song was ""Piano In The Dark by Brenda Russell.

"When I find myself watching the time, I never think about all the funny things you said..."

He'd hum it when he cooked. Play it on vinyl on Sunday mornings while making pancakes. Our love was never smooth. It had dissonance, like a song with too many notes, but it was real. And when it ended, I didn't just lose a man. I lost a muse.

To this day, I still wondered how someone so full of music became a void that I couldn't fill.

And then, like a quiet epilogue of them all, there's Dionne Warwick. And not just one of her songs, but her entire collection. Dionne was always playing in the background during my darkest nights when my emotions tore my ass up. "Walk On By," "Anyone Who Had A Heart," and "Alfie, I'll Never Love This Way Again..." each one became an emotional map of my life's missteps.

Alex, Rick, Farouk, Michael, and Kendrick were more than just my lovers. They were mirrors into my disavowed soul. Vesta Williams, "Congratulations!" Oh, my, my, my. That song was my theme, baby, dealing with those that married women to hide their affairs with me.

Reminders of roads never to travel again. They were my teachers. I said "teachers" because they taught me that maybe men wasn't shit.

We were like the song by Atlantic Starr, "Secret Lovers," I couldn't make it clearer than that.

I'd come to realize that loving someone didn't always mean that you were ready for them. And hurting someone didn't always mean you didn't love them.

Thankfully, I was sixty years old now. And when those

songs play, I didn't rush to turn them off. I let them play.

I let them take me back...to the laughter, the kisses, the tears, and the tearful departures.

The nostalgia nearly crippled me.

Because even if I failed at love, love never failed me. And those songs? They were proof that I was loved by some good men, and burned by them as well.

The grass wasn't always greener, and all gold didn't glitter.

83

Family Ain't Worth Shit

THERE WAS A BIG DIFFERENCE BETWEEN SILENCE and peace. There was a Jamaican saying, "Good friends are better than pocket money," that I lived by. The real meaning was that true friends were better than your own family.

And for years, I stayed silent when it came to the family my grandmother helped raise. Rosemarie's children, all eleven of them. But now, I was choosing to live in peace.

And peace, for me, meant living in my truth. Anything that jeopardized my peace I quietly nipped in the bud.

I couldn't take the good without the bad. My grandmother was a peaceful but strong woman.

She wasn't just my father's mother. She was the matriarch of an estranged family. She was the spine that held it all together. Her sister, Rosemarie, had eleven children, and for reasons I'd never fully understand, my grandmother decided that her only son (my father) would be better off growing up not as an only child, but as the twelfth among them.

She embedded him into that household like one of their

own. He wasn't just their cousin; he was raised like a brother. That decision shaped everything.

While the house was full of children, it was my grandmother's wallet, wisdom, and willpower that paved the way for their futures.

She silently seeded the success of that entire generation. She never bragged about it. Never reminded them of what they owed her.

That wasn't her way. She gave because she believed in giving, and because she loved them.

For instance, take the first niece, Beryl, the eldest of the eleven children. She was the same age as my father and closest to him in spirit.

My grandmother adored her, and when Beryl decided to become a nurse, it was my grandmother who paid her passage and tuition to study in England.

And Beryl never forgot that selfless act.

Of all of them, she was the only one I ever felt a real connection with—the only one who truly carried my grandmother's spirit.

When I was just three months old, brought to the house by Enid (my birth mother) Beryl was the one who examined me, worried that I hadn't been getting the nutrients I needed.

There was no breast milk, and I was already small for my age. It was Beryl who made sure I was fed. She got me Enfamil formula and insisted I be looked after with care.

She may not have known she was looking at her second cousin, but she looked at me with compassion. And that was more than I could say for the rest of them.

When my grandmother died, it was like they had all forgotten who she was.

Forgotten everything that she did for them. Not one of them—*not one*—offered to help with her funeral.

The same woman who had invested in their futures, who had loved them like her own children, and they didn't lift a finger when it mattered the most.

I watched in disbelief as they vanished into the background, silent and smug in their own successes. It was like "Thank you, nigga, but I didn't need you," after gaining the whole world.

They'd become doctors, nurses, administrators, engineers, and hotel managers.

They all had the means, but none of them had a heart. And I would be honest.

I wrestled with my angels and demons writing my

autobiography. I didn't want to sound bitter. I didn't want to come off as vengeful. I didn't want to turn my intimate sexual experiences into smut.

But the truth was, my family was selfish.

They were ungrateful.

They were cruel and always absent from my life. And they proved something to me that I had always suspected but never wanted to believe.

I was never one of them

Technically, I was their second cousin. But they never treated me like family. I wasn't included. I wasn't embraced. I was merely *there*——a ghost in the house my grandmother had built.

Beryl remained different.

Her warmth and her loyalty to my grandmother was unmatched. But even her son, Norman, saw what I saw.

When Beryl passed away, her siblings didn't show up for her. They didn't support her son. And he, like me, chose to walk away.

I didn't realize how far I'd drifted from my family until I saw them in rare form, at their coldest.

Then it hit me like ice water: *I was never part of the inner circle to begin with.*

I'd cut them off.

Completely.

I had no interest in reuniting, reconciling, or pretending we share anything beyond blood. Blood might make you related, but it didn't make you family.

They may have read this chapter, and I hoped that they did.

And if they were offended, then good—it meant the truth finally got through. Because my story wasn't about bitterness.

It was about being a light in someone else's life, a person who might be waiting for a story like mine.

Yes, I'd been around the world and got my wine and dine on in hundreds of countries, but for the first time in my life, I was drawing my future with clarity.

To my grandmother, Aunt Lou. I

carried your love like armor.

You were the light that led so many through the darkness, and they would never dim your legacy, not in my eyes.

I wouldn't allow it.

They may have forgotten what you gave, but I never would.

You deserved a thousand hands to lift you up when you left this world.

But in the end, I was there. I carried the weight. Alone—but

I was honored and proud.

And to the eleven, now eight relatives?

You all can GO TO HELL!

84
What Do I Call Her?

DONNA PICKED ME UP FROM THE AIRPORT, and we drove straight to the family home. As the car hummed along, she filled the silence with stories I wasn't sure I was ready to hear. I literally had to mentally prepare myself to take it all in. She told me how she came to the United States, how she took the surname of the police officer Enid had married in Florida.

Donna was born in 1961, and I was born in 1962. A sister I barely knew guided me toward the woman who had given me life.

We reached the house around four o'clock. Enid didn't get off work until five. That left me an hour to wrestle with my nerves. Donna, sensing my unease, asked gently if I wanted a drink.

"Do you have any Johnnie Walker?" I asked.

She nodded, poured my troubles into a small glass, and I wolfed it down in one greedy gulp, like a starving child clinging to a mother's breast. The warmth spread, but it wasn't enough to drown out my anxiety. She poured me another shot, and I obliged. She could see the storm brewing in me. The house phone rang, startling us. Donna answered: "Yes... he's here." A pause. Then she hung up. I didn't need to be told who it was. My stomach dropped. Enid was on her way.

I sat in the living room, surrounded by framed proof of a family I wasn't a part of. Daughters were in graduation gowns, Donna the track star, medals and trophies glittered like silent accusations. There was even a photo of Enid in her Pan Am flight attendant uniform.

Achievements lined the walls; my absence hung heavier than all of them. I checked my Rolex again and again, as if I were waiting for my own execution. Marie Antoinette in the drawing room. Only this was no guillotine, it was flesh and blood.

I had already booked a hotel room near the airport for the following day. There was no way I was staying in this house. This wasn't a homecoming; it was reconnaissance, in my opinion.

At 5:15, I heard tires biting into the gravel as a car pulled up.

Instantly my chest tightened aggravating my last good nerve. My thoughts collided.

What do I call her? Mummy? No. Enid? Too cold. Should I hug her? Shake her hand? Then the flight attendant in me took over: Smile. Be courteous. Nod. Go with the flow. The chair I sat in directly faced the front door.

The knob turned, and she walked in.

Enid. The woman who carried me for nine months, then left me with my grandmother at age three months. The woman who called my headmaster, Mr. McKay, to announce herself as my mother, detonating the secret that drove me from my family before Paris.

The woman whose chaos had cost my father his job at Pan Am. The troublemaker, or whistleblower.

She was shorter than I had imagined. Her features carried a trace of Indian blood. For a fleeting second, she looked like a seasoned flight attendant herself. Cautiously, she stepped forward towards me. Enid's eyes brimmed with crocodile tears. "Is this my son? My handsome son?"

I smiled, but words deserted me. She opened her arms, and suddenly I was in her grasp. The hug was so tight I couldn't breathe. Her body shook from joy, and her tears flowed freely.

I gently patted her back. "Come, come now," I said softly. "No time for tears. This is a reunion."

I reminded her that I had little time. I was leaving the next morning, checked into an airport hotel. But Enid had other ideas.

She wanted me to meet everybody and their mammy—not just her closest family, but the whole extended web of relatives, cousins twice and thrice removed. They were all waiting to claim a piece of me. I wasn't ready for that circus.

So, I drew a line in the sand: "Let's meet the most important of them all."

Inevitably, I was introduced to her parents—my maternal grandparents—and to Michelle's son, Lloyd. We shared a meal. It was civil and emotional, but beneath every polite exchange was the weight of history pressing down.

Later, Donna drove me back to the hotel. My mind spun like it was on spin cycle.

What a day. I had finally met Enid, the woman at the center of all my beginnings and betrayals.

The one who had given me life, and with it, a legacy of secrets, fractures, and unanswered questions.

This wasn't a fairytale reunion.

EPILOGUE

"Now You Know...
But You Don't Know Everything"

I THOUGHT I HAD SEEN IT ALL. THIRTY YEARS IN THE sky, on private jets, in locker rooms, war zones, aircrafts and penthouses, was definitely a journey. I'd poured champagne for billionaires and held the hand of a soldier flying to his death. I'd kissed a man the world would never let me love out in the open and danced with celebrities who couldn't admit who they were behind closed doors.

I'd kept secrets. I'd carried diamonds. I'd seen men ruin their lives with one rumor. And I'd watched women climb to power on nothing but ambition and stilettos.

You've read the stories (the glory, the heartbreak, the danger, and the betrayal). But the truth: I hadn't told you everything. Not yet. There were names I still hadn't mentioned. Affairs that would shatter marriages. Deals that could land people in prison.

There was a scandal that nearly ruined me, and I haven't written a word about it in these pages.

Why? Because I wasn't finished.

This book was just the takeoff. The real turbulence was in what I hadn't told you yet. The part of the story that never made it to the media...the part where I almost lost everything—my freedom, my career, and my life before I actually did.

But that was a story for another time.

You buckled your seatbelt. You enjoyed the ride. But trust me...the descent was where things get dangerous.

To Be Continued....

Book 2:

The Landing

Coming Soon

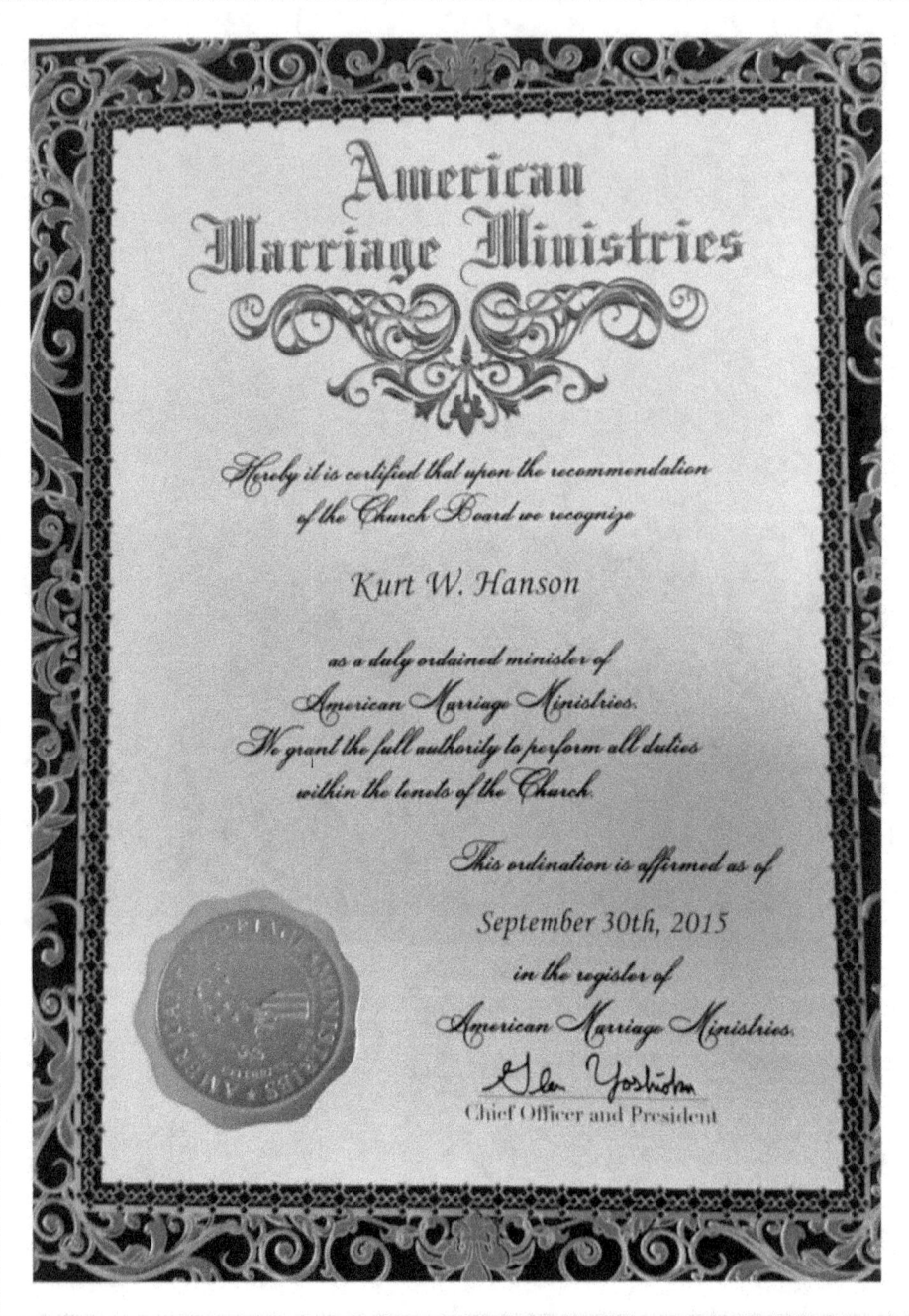

The Reverend Kurt Hanson

"From the skies of the world to the depths of despair, I rose again–because my story was never meant to end in defeat"

Kurt Hanson

ABOUT THE AUTHOR

Kurt Hanson's extraordinary life journey is one of ambition, artistry, faith, and triumph. A proud graduate of Jamaica College, one of Jamaica's top institutions, he earned a coveted scholarship to the prestigious Sorbonne University in Paris, France.

He is an Ordained Minister, a trained Baritone singer who performed with a string quartet of elite Jamaican Philharmonic

Orchestra musicians, a certified Professional in Human Resources (PHR), and holds a master's degree in communications.

For over three decades, Kurt carved out a remarkable career in international aviation, flying across the globe as a distinguished flight attendant.

His career took him to all Seven Wonders of the World and more than a hundred countries worldwide, serving presidents, dignitaries, world-class athletes, and celebrities.

He dined at the White House with the President of the United States, flew alongside the White House press corps, and provided elite service to NBA and NFL teams, including championship legends.

But his story is not only one of glamour, it is also one of resilience.

After losing everything and spending three years homeless, Kurt rebuilt his life with unshakable faith and the grace of God. Today, he is a global ambassador, community leader, and respected voice for homelessness and mental health advocacy, inspiring countless others who believe in the power of perseverance and destiny.

Personal reflections

In Photos

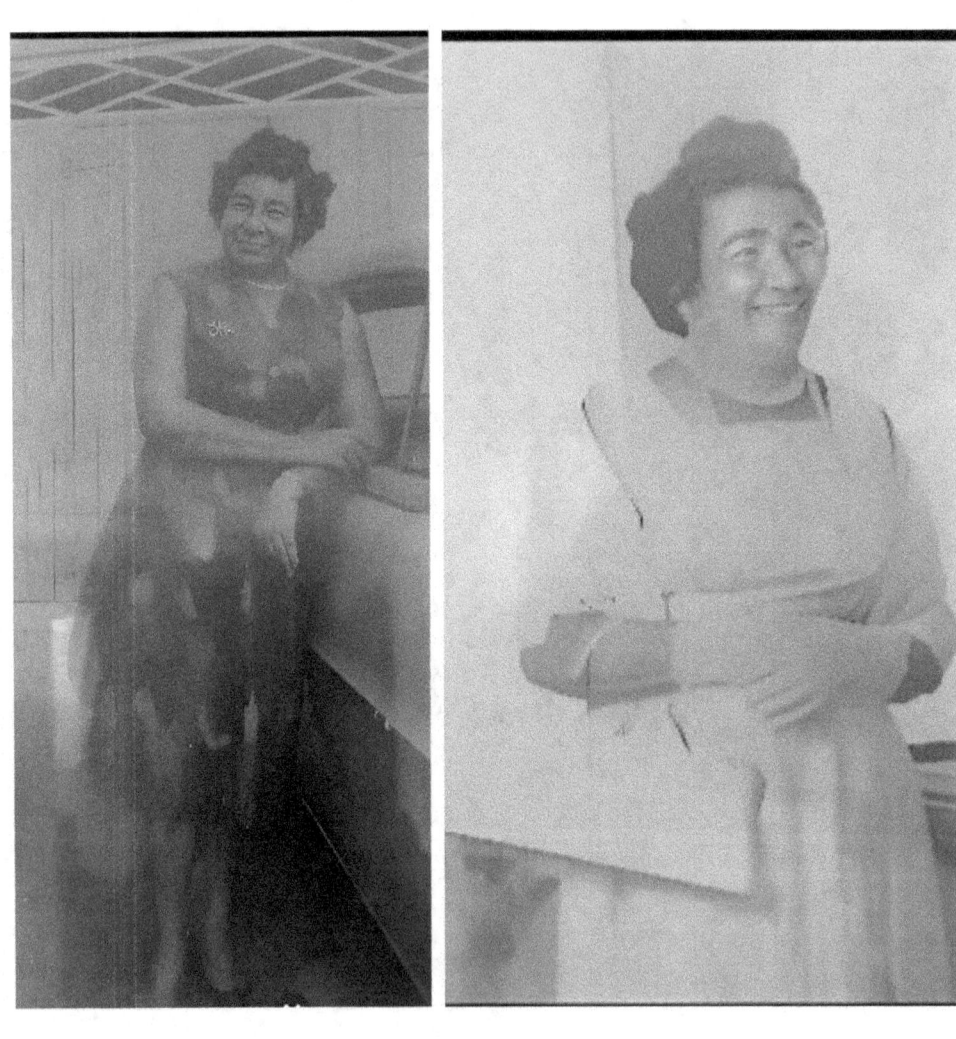

My Grandmother, Leila Louisa "Aunt Lou" Mason. My heart and my soul

329 | Kurt Hanson

Kurt Hanson and Don Lemon

The Gentleman's Ball. Atlanta; Georgia in 2015.
Kurt Hanson, guest speaker.

Larry Wilson Jr. (Dapharoah69), Kurt Hanson & John Wilson

Motown meets Pan-Am Airlines, 1961

Reception at the White House with President Barack Obama

A shared moment with President Barack Obama and Congressman John Lewis

Kurt Hanson and Sean Hayes (Will & Grace)

THE LEGENDARY TONY TERRY AND B ANGIE B

Delta in Flight Pride Parade. 2009. Atlanta, Georgia.

Kurt Hanson at The White House

Moscow, Russia. 2000

Kurt Hanson and Coach Phil Jackson (Chicago Bulls and the L.A. Lakers)

My father at flight school Age 20

Kurt Hanson and Eva Longoria

*Kurt Hanson with his sister
Marcia Barrett of Boney M and her
husband Marcus James*

*Kurt Hanson and Andy Cohen from
Bravo TV Housewives*